WOMEN ON THE MOVE:

A Christian Perspective on Cross-Cultural Adaptation

GRETCHEN JANSSEN

INTERCULTURAL PRESS, INC.

For information, contact:
Intercultural Press, Inc.
P.O. Box 700
Yarmouth, ME 04096, USA

Book design by Meg McMullen
Cover design by LetterSpace
Printed in the United States of America.
97 96 95 94 93   3 4 5 6 7

Library of Congress Cataloging-in-Publication Data

Janssen, Gretchen.
    [Women overseas]
    Women on the move: a Christian perspective on cross-cultural adaptation/by Gretchen Janssen.
        p. cm.
    Previously published as: Women overseas. © 1989.
    Includes bibliographical references.
    ISBN 1-877864-09-0:
    1. Wives—Religious life.   2. Cross-cultural orientation.
3. Culture shock.   4. Christianity and culture.   I. Title.
BV4527.J38   1992
248.8'435—dc20   91-43918
                                                        CIP

Dedication

To my husband Jerry and our sons Andrew and Matthew with whom I have made these moves through which we all have learned much.

Table of Contents

Acknowledgments

I am grateful to God for the gift of faith without which this book would never have been written, and to all those who continue to shape my faith through the way they live. I am thankful to Gien Karssen and Kathy Yanni, who encouraged me in the beginning writing stages and to Intercultural Press, specifically to David and Kay Hoopes, who believed in the value of this book and to Peggy Pusch and Judy Carl Hendrick for the editing, which has made it a better book than I ever could have done on my own. My thanks also to Carol Walker and to Faith Pushee, who typed and retyped the manuscript. And finally, I especially want to say thank you to all the women who have been willing to share their life experiences with me. This book is a culmination of our joint efforts to find meaning in our lives. As God said, "Behold I am doing a new thing; now it springs forth, do you not perceive it?" (Isaiah 43:19)

Foreword

I have never met Gretchen Janssen but she helped me through a hard time. That's why I know she can help you too. My husband was ambassador to the Netherlands from 1983-86. Gretchen had already left, but the good she did continued on. She reached me through an article that she had written about moving for the American Women's Club magazine.

Like many other newcomers in a strange environment I was miserable and so was my family. You might think such a move is easier for an ambassador's wife who has all the support systems of a ready-made house and staff, but just the opposite is true. As ambassador's wife you have to be "on" from the moment you get off the plane. You can't hide away until you get your bearings or your sense of humor back. You and your family are on public display from the beginning. I thought that I was ready for this after twenty years in the foreign service but for two reasons I wasn't. First, I had never, in our rather long career, known a happy ambassador's wife. I had no good role models. And, secondly, my children, who were just entering puberty when we moved, were acutely unhappy. Our son acted out his anger and our daughter cried herself to sleep every night. My husband, like yours, threw himself into his new job.

One day I happened to pick up a copy of the American Women's club magazine. An article on "Beginnings and Endings" caught my eye and then I saw the wonderful words from Isaiah that Gretchen quoted, "Remember not the former things nor consider the things of old. Behold I am doing a new thing. Now it springs forth; do you not perceive it." These words were like a balm to my soul. I read them to my children and they seemed to feel their comforting effects too. Slowly, from that time we began not only to heal but to grow and flourish in our "new thing".

Now Gretchen Janssen has put her advice and wisdom into this book. What makes it special is what made that article I read special. Not only does it contain good practical, human, woman-to-woman suggestions but it is built on a foundation of God's healing words. Perhaps you are already a believer, perhaps you aren't. It makes no difference. If you are anticipating a move, or have just made a move, you are experiencing stress. You need help, just as I did. Other people can help you, this book can help you, but the one who can help you the most is the one who can heal where it hurts the most—in your spirit—and that one is God. Try Him and His words. He'll turn your pain into joy and Gretchen Janssen will show you the way, just as she showed me.

Frances Bremer
Author of *Coping With His Success*

Introduction

This book is intended to be a guide for wives who accompany their husbands and families in major geographical moves. It will be found valuable both by women moving overseas and by those moving within their home countries. It is designed to be used for individual reflection or in small groups as a stimulus to discussion; the exercises that are included work either way.

This book approaches moving to another cultural setting from a Christian perspective although it can also be valuable to those with other beliefs. Women can sort through and understand the range of transitions involved in moving and develop a fuller awareness and acceptance of this time as an integral and valuable part of their spiritual journey. This aspect of moving has, in my opinion, rarely been addressed; however, it is precisely the issue which needs to be dealt with so maximum benefit can be derived from the transitional experience. I have come to realize that moves may be God's call to me to go forth into a new period of growth in relationship with God and to become all that God envisions me to be as a woman responsible to God in my human relationships.

Women On The Move is valuable if you read it before you move as a preview of what's in store for you. Chapter 3 on culture shock will be particularly useful in helping you understand the normal process of cross-cultural adaptation. If you have some idea of what to expect, it will not be such a surprise (or shock) when you go through the moods and reactions which you experience living in a new and different environment.

But you will gain the greatest value from this book after you have arrived at your destination and face the necessity of assessing new opportunities and sorting through priorities as you adapt to the resources available to you. As your lifestyle is shaken up, new goal setting will be a must but can only be done effectively when you are on site.

I will not discuss such logistical issues as how to cope with money, transportation, food, finding cleaning help or other such matters of daily life. There are many fine books which provide that kind of information, and some are listed in the bibliography and resource list I have included. Instead, it is my intent to help you approach your move as a valuable part of your life and to provide you with the tools to tap your own inner resources in managing it. You will then know what additional external resources you need to make this one of the most meaningful experiences you will ever have.

To gain the most benefit from this book, I suggest you share the experience of reading it with a friend or group of friends. The sharing and discussion that result will increase its value and will also deepen your relationships. The development of strong friendships has been shown to be one of the most important ways in which women on the move can give, and receive, mutually needed support. Whether alone or together with friends, read each chapter carefully and work through the exercises found at the end. Actually doing the exercises will help you work through the feelings and issues of transition systematically rather than just thinking about them. You will reap a far richer benefit by engaging in this process.

What I have written is based on my personal experiences and those of other women. Everyone experiences a major move differently, but there is much that is shared. I have known the feelings of excitement, frustration, anger, and joy that you have or will experience. Although the transitions and adjustments seemed unbearably difficult at times, looking back, our family would never give them up. We have only begun to appreciate the many ways they have contributed to our growth both as individuals and in relationship to each other.

I pray God will meet you through these pages in which I share with you what I have learned through my experiences and those of other women.

Gretchen White Janssen

Since the original publication of this book in 1989 under the title *Women Overseas,* I have become increasingly aware of its value for women who move from city to city or from region to region within their own country. I have also learned that the concepts presented here can provide valuable insights into inner moves and transitions required during life changes, such as returning to work after years of homemaking; experiencing divorce; the death of a spouse; the empty-nest syndrome; and so on. Finally, I have seen the value of the exercises included below for women in the process of self-discovery through psychotherapy. Like any other journey we undertake, inner change requires changes in our attitudes, beliefs, expectations and actions. I believe this book can be helpful.

G.W.J.

one
―――

In the Beginning

LOOKING BACKWARD

It is funny how things fall into place–like a pattern that emerges in a kaleidoscope which has been turned around and around. So it was one afternoon as I prepared a Bible study program for my thirteen-year-old son's Bible Club.

Our family was in the middle of a four-year assignment in The Netherlands following two years in Denmark. It had been hard for me to leave a half-finished seminary degree program when we embarked on the first assignment. I had finally become a full-time student after several years of part-time study and fitting classes around caring for two small boys, a big dog, and a house while my husband traveled on business two-thirds of the time. Although I had always believed that God must have a plan to explain the disruption of moving in my life, I had no idea what it was. Then, while preparing my son's Bible study, I ran across a little vignette which finally provided a clear image of that plan. Indeed, the story spoke so directly to me it seemed to jump off the page:

A friend of mine, spending a few days in the neighborhood of our English lakes, came upon the most beautiful shrubs he had ever seen. Arrested by their extraordinary luxuriance, he learned that it was due to a judicious system of transplanting, constantly pursued. Our heavenly Father is constantly transplanting us. And these changes, if they are rightly accepted, result in the most exquisite manifestation of Christian character and experience.[1]

"Aha!" I thought, "So that's what God (I hope) is doing in my life. There is a reason for all this transplantation!" At that moment, I realized God truly must be in charge.

As I laid aside the Bible Club preparations and began to reflect on my life, I realized that my husband's job transfers from California to New Jersey, then to Denmark and The Netherlands, and ultimately back to New Jersey actually formed a pattern. Each move played a significant role in the spiritual growth that had begun when I made a serious commitment to Jesus Christ. In every location I met new people and encountered new opportunities which were vital to the growth and development of my relationship with God. I thought again of Acts 17:26-27:

> And God made from one every nation of people to live on all the face of the earth, having determined allotted periods and the boundaries of their habitation that they should seek God, in the hope that they might feel after God and find God.

Although I knew and had quoted these verses to others, I realized I had never really appropriated them for my own life or that of my family. Could it mean that God had determined where we would live and for how long, expressly for the purpose and with the hope that we should seek and find God in that place? This would mean that God was totally involved in all our moves so that through them we would experience God in new ways. It was startling, and at the same time it made perfect sense. Just like the transplanted shrubs, I too was being replanted by God, the master gardener.

Each transplantation involves a shock to the system and temporary setbacks. I had certainly experienced those. But as with plants, new growth follows, and these insights led directly to a new approach to future moves. Although my husband, Jerry, and I had prayed about the moves, committing ourselves to God's keeping, we were now firm in our belief that indeed our moves were according to God's plan.

I was exhilarated as I began to look back at my life with this new perspective. I was eight years old when I asked Jesus Christ to be Lord of my life. Miss Anita Lake, an elderly Christian missionary, moved into our neighborhood and invited my best friend, June, and me to meet weekly in a "club" for Bible study, prayer, singing, and crafts. In that context, as an eight-year-old girl from a nominally Christian family, I committed myself to Jesus Christ. I wrote the date, April 8, 1948, in front of the New Testament Miss Lake gave me on that occasion.

There were a lot of years between that day and another day early in June 1972 when I "abandoned" my life to Jesus Christ as Lord. That act, taken just before my thirty-third birthday, meant something very different to me from the commitment I had made as a child. Until then it seemed I had everything my upbringing told me was important–health, a college degree, many and varied interests, a handsome husband, two beautiful children, and a lovely home in La Jolla, California, known locally as "heaven on earth." What more, by the standards of this world, could I possibly want? I went to church and called myself a Christian. But then I entered a long and deep depression. My life seemed empty, void of focus and direction. I was so busy trying to be what I thought I "should" be or what others expected of me that I had lost touch with my own self. I saw some people in our church who were alive in a joyful way–a way I was well aware I was not. Their lives and relationships were of a different quality than I had ever experienced. I longed to be alive as they were, and I began to pray that I would become "a woman of God." Things got worse—much worse—until I even considered ending my own life. One day I was reading a small book by Lloyd Ogilvie (*A Life Full of Surprises*) in which he talked about abandoning your life to Christ, and I realized that I had not turned the control of my life over to God. I debated. Who was God anyway? Was God worthy of my trust for such an enormous step? There were many things in my life about which I felt bitter. Our house in La Jolla was on the edge of a canyon filled with weeds and shrubs to which the children and I were allergic, so we were constantly sick. My parents were in the throes of a painful divorce. Jerry's job was difficult and stressful. I was an angry young woman. But slowly and patiently a few Christian friends listened and cared for me and gradually, for one of the first times in my life, I felt loved just for who I was. It dawned on me one day that God must love like that too, loving us just for who we are. And I took the risk, the big leap of faith, and said yes to God. I gave myself, all I was then and all I would ever be, to God. Life became life with a capital "L" and I began to experience the promise of abundant life. No sooner, it seemed, did I risk reaching out to Christ than we learned we were to move to the east coast. I couldn't believe it! I had always lived in Southern California. The East was so far away, and everyone said it was a cold and unfriendly place. How could I leave California and this new way of life which meant so much to me?

It was in this first move that I learned God had gone before us, preparing the way for me to be able to grow in a closer relationship with the living Lord. New friends and new opportunities to use my skills and abilities brought me more fulfillment than I'd had in California. Yet, there were days when I longed for my friends back home, and it was one such day when I heard Jesus' words, "No one who puts the hand to the plow and looks back is fit for the kingdom of God" (Luke 9:62). I was looking back. Not fit for the kingdom of God? I suddenly realized if I were to keep looking back and comparing our new church and new experiences to those we had had in the past, I would miss the new opportunities God was offering us here. From that moment Isaiah 43:18-19 became a touchstone: "Remember not the former things, nor consider the things of old. Behold I am doing a new thing; now it springs forth, do you not perceive it?" I consciously opened myself to the new possibilities that God would reveal in our new home.

God truly blessed us. We found friends with whom we developed more caring and deeper relationships than we had ever known. They were the kinds of relationships I had longed for. We found a church family where we both gave and received much nurture. I enjoyed teaching classes in Parent Effectiveness Training and began work at Union Theological Seminary in New York with the intention of some day enrolling full-time in the master of divinity program. For one of the first times in my life I felt fully integrated.

This wonderful life lasted four years, and I, of course, could not imagine anything better. Then Jerry came home one day and told me we might move to Denmark, and the questions all came back again. Why were we to move? After four years of one or two courses a semester I had officially enrolled full-time in the master's program at Union. My cup was running over. What was God doing anyway? Since the Old Testament is full of prophets arguing with God, I decided if they could do it, so could I. I yelled and shook my fist and asked what God had in mind. It was fine for Jerry, I said, but not for me. I even considered all possible alternatives–staying behind with the children, staying behind alone, divorce. In the meantime we had no timetable. How long before we would leave for Denmark? Should I enroll for spring courses or not? I decided to go ahead and take all the courses I could. Despite the uncertainty, I believed during this time that God must have a plan even though it was certainly not clear to me. It was the day I turned in my last paper that Jerry called from the office and said he was to go to Denmark as soon as possible. I did not yet know it, but God's timing was perfect. I was soon going to need all the courses I had taken.

What a wonderful experience Denmark turned out to be! I served as assistant pastor at the American Church in Copenhagen, an internship for which I received credit at the seminary. That was a bonus and a challenging opportunity I had never expected. I could put into practice some of the ideas to which

I had been exposed and also became very aware of areas in which I needed much more knowledge and experience.

THE WIFE'S DILEMMA

After two years in Denmark, instead of returning to the States, as originally planned, we moved again, this time to The Netherlands. Again, my plans for continued study had to be postponed. But at the same time I found that I was learning something very important. I had observed the women and families around me adapting in different ways to new countries, lifestyles and situations. Some had moved often and knew what to expect, where and how to get involved and create a meaningful experience for themselves. They "knew the ropes," so to speak, partly because they knew themselves and their own needs and gifts. Others floundered and moved through the phases of cross-cultural adaptation with more difficulty. I fell somewhere between the two groups, sometimes floundering and struggling, sometimes managing with unexpected aplomb. As I reflected on what I could see taking place in others and how I experienced my own adaptation process, I began to see differences in how a move to a new country affects the members of the family. Husbands, for the most part, are almost immediately assimilated into their new jobs, where specific assignments and roles provide them with an identity and a support system, and because the new jobs demand major expenditures of energy, they often become totally preoccupied with their work. Children attend school, which often involves difficult adjustments but also provides new tasks, activities and friends, and a framework in which their social and personal identity needs can be met. For wives it is different. They face a situation that is both a dilemma and an opportunity.

Although all family members experience problems and must make adjustments, it is the wife who enters this new living environment shorn almost completely of her previous roles and support systems. Except for her family she has little to help her bridge the gap. At the same time, looking back on my experience, I have come to believe that it is the wives who have the greatest opportunity to reassess their lives and either affirm choices made previously or make new ones and pursue new directions.

Adaptation is a major challenge for a wife, for there is much to disorient her and contribute to her experiencing culture shock. She is in a new culture, country, lifestyle, and home. She may not have the energy, desire or money to decorate her home (which is often a rented one) as she did in her own country, to make it a comfortable place reflecting her personality and identity. She is usually the family member who has to deal with the grocer, the butcher, the plumber, or the repairperson. These encounters, routine but often frustrating even at home, loom as forbidding obstacles in a foreign country with different customs and a different language.

Paddy Welles, a psychologist, author and wife of an executive based in Paris for several years, is writing a book about her experience and says that culture shock is often "the feeling of changing from a competent, functioning, more or less efficient person to someone who is not sure how to buy a head of lettuce at the market or call a plumber." She goes on to say that the first time she read "Bloom Where You Are Planted," an article on orientation to living overseas which is used in an extensive orientation program developed by the American Church in Paris, she didn't know whether to laugh or cry because she immediately pictured herself as the "blooming idiot."[2] I was comforted to know that she too had felt that way because when I met Paddy Welles, I knew I was in the presence of a vital, articulate, self-directed woman. Her experience confirmed the theory that wives are pretty much left to their own devices to find their way through the adaptation process.

Other factors enter the picture. To make new friends takes time—time for trust and a meaningful relationship to develop. I've heard many, many women say, "I know I'm going to be there only a year, and it will hurt so much when I leave that I'm not going to even try to make close friends." Also, if a wife has a career or is in the midst of further education, as I was, her plans have to be modified, adjusted, or terminated. Paid employment is usually not available overseas without a work permit, which can only rarely be obtained, and different social systems may preclude opportunities for volunteerism as we know it in the U.S. You can feel angry and resentful, but you can also face the challenge and find alternate channels through which to express yourself—channels which may open up more opportunities than you ever had before. Once you are ready for new opportunities, I am convinced you will find them.

Leisure activities, sports, clubs, or travel often fill in the gap although even these may be different from what you enjoyed at home, and you may have to be more adventuresome to try some of them. You join local groups and encounter a language barrier which needs to be overcome. Long before aerobics was popular in the States, I learned to "follow the leader" in aerobics classes given only in Danish. Becoming an active participant in the community requires more than language acquisition, however. There are new customs, ways of developing relationships, and styles of communicating to learn.

On the other hand, if you join English-speaking groups, because of the transient nature of most expatriate communities, you are quickly drawn in and become part of it, often developing new relationships which evolve into lasting friendships. I am constantly amazed at how these seemingly temporary friendships continue through letters and unexpected opportunities to see each other again. We recently visited Australia to spend time with one of our son's best friends from The Netherlands. Even as I write this chapter, we are anticipating a visit from close Dutch friends.

Spurred by my own experiences, I began research on what the needs of expatriate women are and what happens to them when they move to a new environment. I will share with you what I have learned from both a practical and a spiritual viewpoint and describe how my life has been transformed during the moving experiences into a wonderfully exciting and deepening awareness of God's influence on my life. Hopefully, you will be stirred to seek a new awareness of God's guiding presence in your own life.

Questions, exercises, and Bible studies are included in each chapter of this book. I encourage you to take the time to do them so that the material presented will come alive for you personally. If you do them before your move, be ready to return to the book after you've settled and do them again. I've known women who have used them a number of times in adjusting to moves not only overseas but from one part of the U.S. to another. I have done them many times, not the least important of which was upon our return to the States after six years overseas. They were particularly helpful as I thought through the question, "Do I want to continue in the pursuit of a seminary degree or not?" As I went through the exercises, defining new goals and needs and deciding what activities to participate in (selecting only those which were relevant to the goals and needs I identified), I discovered I was unreservedly happy. Later, I discovered how unusual it was to be able to manage reentry so well.

Reentry adjustment is a major problem for many people, and we heard many tales of woe from families who were miserable and couldn't readjust to the States when they returned. I rejoiced when following my own advice made a difference.

In the Introduction I have described some possible ways of sharing your experience with others. It is my prayer that you will hear God's voice speaking to you more clearly wherever you are in transition and that your awareness of God's presence within you will increase. As one woman living overseas expressed, "I came to realize that God is the one and only part of my life I can depend on. Everything else is changing all the time." Wherever you are, whether it's Houston, Texas or Lagos, Nigeria, God is there with you. You can count on it!

two
___

The Woman's Story

A PROFILE OF WIVES ON THE MOVE

If you are like most wives experiencing a new culture or living environment, you find yourself wondering, especially when you are in a low period, why you seem to be the only one with problems. Is there anyone else sharing this boat? In fact nearly everyone **does** experience difficulties though few admit it. Wives feel a great responsibility for holding the family together during this time and often hide their own problems and anxieties. More than one woman has told me, "If I fall apart, who will hold us together?"

Listening to the thoughts and feelings of others and knowing my own experiences led me to explore the needs of women making cross-cultural moves. My goal was to learn what they had experienced, what had been easy or difficult in their transition, and what had worked to their advantage and what had not. I also looked for the benefits derived from the transition. The first step was to interview married women who had moved to The Netherlands in recent years. Then a questionnaire was developed (see complete copy in the appendix) which was ultimately distributed to 344 women living in twelve countries. Only married women were surveyed. My assumption was that they experienced this time of change differently from single women. At a return rate of 58 percent, 200 completed questionnaires were received. From them we can draw some conclusions and observe some trends.

Not all women who responded were Americans, but all were women now living in countries other than their own. The majority had been married between twelve and eighteen years and most had completed more than two years of college. Why had they moved? The results were not surprising.

85% had moved because of the husband's job
7% had moved because of marriage
8% had moved for other reasons (e.g., joint
    assignments, a wife's career)

What was their living abroad experience? Nearly half the group had more than one overseas move.

72% of the families had been in Europe three years or less
48% had lived overseas before
52% had never lived outside their own countries before

When asked to define their primary life concerns, the respondents emphasized three areas:

Personal development	35%
Family issues	29%
Adjustment issues	15%
Religion	4%
Other issues	17%

Many women found it necessary to rethink their goals and life direction as a result of moving into a situation where their roles and activities were changed. While moves within one's own country may have a similar effect, there are enough familiar aspects of the culture and environment to ease the impact and allow one to transfer skills and roles. In a completely different culture, there is likely to be much less that is familiar and far fewer opportunities for transferring skills and roles, and that poses a problem.

SEEING GOD AS PART OF OUR MOVE

During my family's first overseas move, I thought I had intellectually and even emotionally reached the point where I believed that God had a purpose although I did not yet know or see it. I still cried out, "I believe. Help thou my unbelief" (see Mark 9:14-29). I needed Jesus' healing touch for the vestiges of doubt and unbelief. As we sat in church the first Sunday, a short story (told by the pastor) provided me with a new insight:

> A father, carrying his small blind son, met a friend one day on the street. While they were talking, the friend asked to hold the boy in his arms. After they had left, the father asked his son if he had been afraid when his friend had taken him in his arms. 'No, Daddy. I knew you wouldn't have given me to him unless he was a friend you trusted with me.'

The boy's reply struck home. Suddenly I realized we would not have been brought to Denmark unless God knew and trusted the country and the environment. I was blind to the purposes behind the move and to the opportunities yet to be discovered, but my belief that God was there with us at that moment was reaffirmed.

God knows where we are—whether it is in the heights of joy, the depths of despair, or somewhere in between. Look again at Psalms 139:

> Lord, you have examined me
>   and you know me.
> You know everything I do.
>   From far away you understand all my thoughts.

You see me whether I am working or resting.
You know all my actions.
Even before I speak, you know
already what I will say.
You are all around me on every side.
You protect me with your power.
Your knowledge of me is too deep.
It is beyond my understanding.
Where could I go to escape from you?
Where could I get away from your presence?
If I went up to heaven you would be there.
If I lay down in the world of the
dead you would be there.
If I flew away beyond the east or
lived in the farthest place in the west
You would be there to lead me.
You would be there to help me.
I could ask the darkness to hide me or
the light round me to turn into night,
but even the darkness is not dark for you,
and the light is as bright as the day.
Darkness and light are the same to you.

(Today's English Version)

I realized God had prepared me for what God had prepared **for** me. More importantly, God was there to lead and help me. Our vulnerability as we search for new meaning within an unfamiliar context is perhaps God's way of getting our attention, pulling at us, asking us to move into a new depth of relationship with our Lord.

Family life may be enhanced by the sense of togetherness which arises from the necessity to be a cohesive unit in new surroundings. Advisors stress, however, that families already in trouble should not undertake such a drastic change. The strain on relationships can be too much. The concern expressed by questionnaire respondents about stabilizing and knitting families together in the midst of new situations indicates the presence of such stress. But for families already relating well, it can be a time of deepening appreciation and growth.

GROWTH AS A RESULT OF MOVING

Asked to name the areas in which they experienced the most growth as a result of the move, the respondents indicated the primary benefit to be personal growth. They developed a greater understanding and appreciation of other cultures and countries. They also became more knowledgeable and broadened their interest areas through experiences in the new environment and through travel to historical and cultural sites. Several commented that they had learned many new skills they would never have learned at home (folk dancing in Norway, *hinderlopen* painting in Holland, appreciation of Oriental carpets in Turkey, etc.). New, unforeseen opportunities replaced old familiar ones and most women increased the level and breadth of their skills; they also discovered new activities and assumed new roles that were rewarding and satisfying.

The women listed the **qualities** they had developed abroad: "learning to balance individual life and family life," "reevaluating personal goals and future life direction," "discerning God's will," "increased independence and the ability to make the best of difficult situations," "becoming aggressive in order to cope better," "learning that other ways, not just the American way, make sense," and "increased self-confidence and feelings of self-worth." One person wrote: "I have gained insight into my own abilities, limitations and flexibility as well as into the rigidity of my thoughts and ideas; improved self-awareness and self-understanding."

But it must be noted that many, many women wrote that these qualities did not magically blossom. They were the slow-maturing fruits of "being forced into new situations," "learning to cope," and "wrestling with new and perplexing experiences." The circumstances are a stimulus to increased self-understanding, one of the qualities necessary to transforming difficulties into opportunities.

A few people responded to this question with negative comments: "It is a forced vacation because I cannot pursue my career." Another woman wrote that she had experienced not growth, but suspension of herself and her personal relationships to support her husband and children away from familiar anchors. My own initial reaction was anger because I had to leave work important to me.

Almost everyone experiences frustration resulting from changes in identities, roles, and support systems. When we are able to release the situation and its control to God, we are able to grow beyond our old limits into more of the person God has created us to be as we open ourselves to new options and experiences.

THE GROWTH OF FAITH IN A MOVE

Because so many of the questionnaires were distributed through nonreligious groups, I was surprised to discover that two-thirds of the respondents rated "religious activities" as the most satisfying of the activities in which they were involved (even though they spent twice as much time in nonreligious activities connected with clubs, schools, community organizations, etc.) Twenty-one percent of the respondents indicated they spent more time engaged in religious activities abroad than they had at home, which suggests that the church has a unique opportunity to reach out and care for these women and their families—to minister to them and also to challenge them. Of the women involved in religious activities, most indicated they had grown in faith in God. One person stated very clearly, "I found my faith in God here." One of the rich opportunities for the overseas church is to reach out to persons who come to church primarily for the fellowship of other English-speaking persons. They are surprised to find God too. Affirming that the family of God is strong, caring, and loving can be a new experience for many.

THE CHALLENGE TO THE CHURCH COMMUNITY

Not everyone has a positive church experience, however. Some people told stories of how they had first reached out to the church with the expectation of caring and warmth which did not materialize. One woman reported that upon arrival in town they got in touch immediately with the church and were invited to a coffee hour. Everyone was friendly; some even took their names and the name of the hotel where they were staying, but no one called or followed up that initial contact. No one knew when she became sick and had a miscarriage, or when the children developed problems in school, or when her husband totaled the car in an accident. No friendly advice was available when they could not find a house to rent. Her initial excitement about the move turned into despair. She became convinced something was terribly wrong with her because she "couldn't adjust!"

This story reminded me how important it is for each of us to be sensitive to others and then to do something about it. It doesn't matter how the word of someone's need spreads, but one or two people calling, helping with shopping, just visiting, listening, and caring can make all the difference in the world. Remembering how people reached out to me reminds me to take a few moments from my schedule and reach out to someone else. It always strikes me anew that Jesus (in Matthew 25:31-46) talks about God's judgment based on how we respond to *human needs:* hunger, thirst (I interpret this not just as physical hunger and thirst, but also psychological, intellectual, emotional, and spiritual hunger), loneliness, illness, and the need for human companionship and comfort. These are common needs to which we all have the capacity to respond.

Any process of change, such as that necessitated by moving overseas, renders us vulnerable. It is an in-between time and Robert Raines, in his book *To Kiss the Joy*, illustrates with the metaphor of a crab shedding its shell. Until a new shell is formed the creature is without protection and is very vulnerable.[3] This description fits women moving overseas. At the same time that we are fragile and unprotected, we are also searching and open. Because this growth is painful and familiar surroundings and supports have been lost, many of us do reach out to the church, perhaps for the first time. The church can meet some of our needs by providing small workshops or discussion groups focused on adjustment issues. Over 70 percent of the respondents to the questionnaire indicated they would like to participate (or had participated) in such groups during their first year abroad. People stressed that it is important that these workshops be open, informal and nonthreatening, "not like a Sunday school class where I would feel embarrassed to ask dumb questions," as one respondent wrote. Also, the discussion leaders must be as open and honest as the participants.

These needs are also shared by wives of pastors serving overseas. They experience the same process of seeking new meaning. Some have found it by more deeply sharing in their husband's work while helping to develop a special ministry to women. One wife expressed this in a talk given at the annual gathering of the Association of Churches in Europe and the Middle East:

> I have felt much more of a call to work as Tom's partner since we've been overseas. There seem to be so many women in our overseas churches who are seeking cultural experiences as well as what to do with their time abroad. I feel myself a much more valuable member of the community than I ever have before.[4]

Two hundred clergy and lay leaders recently surveyed by the Lutheran Church of America stated that one of the highest priorities for the church in the next decade was for the congregation to become a community for mutual support, care, and personal growth.[5] This is needed overseas even more than at home. The Lutheran study also indicated that church dropouts tended to be those who did not feel cared for, loved or wanted. If Jesus commands us to love our neighbor as ourselves, how do we do this so it is felt? Caring and love are experienced one to one. Sixty-two percent of the women in my survey said that *individuals*—not the church, the school or the women's club—were the most important help to them during their time of transition adjustment. While the organizations provided a place for individuals to meet and develop relationships, it is "people caring for people on a one-to-one basis that makes the most difference." One respondent said: "It is the little things that make a difference—someone to smile, to listen, to want to know me as a friend, to try to understand what I am feeling instead of telling me, 'You'll feel better soon,' when I wonder how I will ever feel happy again."

We all live in different neighborhoods, belong to different groups and circles. Wherever we are, there are those around us to whom we can make a difference. We need to ask God to give us a special sensitivity to others **and** a willingness to take the time to be available, even if we cannot do it to perfection. It will be a long time before I forget reading a letter in which one person wrote:

> Christian community is terribly important. It is probably the one *stable* place that is *reality* in an unreal setting. Being uprooted over and over and over is not *natural*. When there is no one who will smile and say, "Hi, Mrs._____," as you are 5,000 miles from home, surrounded by disorder and packing crates, and sometimes unhappy children because no one *knows* you or cares if you live or die, you desperately need Christian community. The minute a man goes in the door of his office in a new region, he has identity. Women have no identity or community for maybe three years, or at least two. But to be able to come to a church where you can say, "I'm Carolyn. I'm a Christian, and I love the Lord," you do have an identity wherever you go. You have a family to which you belong. That's one of the exciting factors about being a Christian.[6]

THE IMPORTANCE OF CARING

As I read this letter, I stopped to think about the importance of caring individually, on a one-to-one basis. At that moment I was trying to collate all the answers to the questionnaires. I suddenly realized I had not yet said hello to my new neighbor who had just moved to The Netherlands from Texas. What a hypocrite! Chagrined, I stopped, and asked her over to have a cup of coffee and meet a few neighbors. What fun we had chatting and laughing as we got to know each other, she taking a break from her packing boxes, and I from my questionnaires. I realized again that is often the little things that speak the loudest. We are known not by what we say but by what we **do**. It may be that by **doing** we will encourage someone else. One person wrote, "The kindnesses shown by others rekindled kindness in me." I have often prayed that someone like that would reach out to the unknown woman who wrote that she had retreated after innumerable moves and was too tired to try anymore.

As we embody this caring for one another we become agents of God's grace and love. No one else may know or care about our pasts or about what is happening now or how we feel, but through our common bond of trust and love in Jesus Christ we can make each other feel welcome and loved.

EXERCISE

This exercise, designed for those already overseas, can help you get in touch with the kinds of emotions you have felt since your arrival abroad. As you reflect on them, you may see ways that you can **intentionally** create opportunities for the more meaningful moments to happen.

Try to remember the **strongest** emotion you felt before coming: excitement? fear? If you are working with a group, discuss the question with a partner. If you are working alone write it down.

_____

_____

_____

Then think of one of the lowest moments you have had since you came overseas. Discuss that with your partner or write it down.

_____

_____

_____

Now think of one of the most meaningful times since you came. Why was it meaningful? What were the ingredients (who, how, what)? Did it have any relationship to God?

_____

_____

_____

How can the church or other groups facilitate the occurrence of more moments? How can you personally bring them about such for yourself, your family, others? If you are working alone, write down your thoughts as completely as you can. If you are in a group, share your thoughts with your partner and the other group members.

_____

_____

_____

three

Culture Shock and Adaptation

How often have you heard warnings such as, "Be ready for culture shock" or "Cross-cultural adaptation is difficult"? What do these terms mean? What is it that you can expect to experience? The aim of this chapter is to define and outline the process of cross-cultural adaptation so that you understand it better, can identify where you are in the process, and can develop ways to manage it successfully and derive the greatest benefit from the opportunities inherent in living in another culture or city.

CULTURE SHOCK—A DEFINITION

Culture shock has been defined as the disorientation caused by the encounter with differing ways of thinking, behaving, and communicating that occur when you move to another cultural environment. It results from being deprived of familiar customs, cues, and meanings in your everyday life and having to deal with ways that are not only unfamiliar but also reflect basic values and assumptions which are different.[7] Practically speaking, this means all the taken-for-granted ways of behaving which are learned or absorbed in growing up and which are followed unconsciously within a given culture: how you greet people; whether you shake hands, hug or kiss; what a smile means; what subjects are appropriate to discuss in what situations; how you negotiate a contract or what a contract is; what you define as right and wrong; and many, many more.

Culture shock can also occur when moving **within** a country, from one region or state to another. As you move from culture to culture, whether country to country or region to region within a country, and whether for the first time or the tenth, you will find the same dynamics in operation as you go through the adaptation process.

UNCONSCIOUS PRECONCEPTIONS

A good first step in adapting to another country is to become aware of the stereotypes of its people you may already hold. For example, if you were moving to The Netherlands, as we did, you would think of words and phrases that reflect your preconceptions about The Netherlands and the Dutch people. Here are some examples voiced by participants in a workshop I conducted:

thrifty
industrious, hard working
religious
neat, clean
friendly, smiling
creative
wear wooden shoes
travelers, explorers
spring flowers, tulips
Dutch cheese

People from other countries, of course, stereotype us too. We all form our opinions based on the information available to us and our information is normally second hand. It comes from what we have read or from the movies or news media, and it is usually an inaccurate representation of reality. One of the worst things about these kinds of preconceptions and stereotypes is that they tend to prevent us from getting to know the people we have stereotyped.

Try making a list of stereotypes of Americans. Here is a list composed by people in The Netherlands about people in the U.S.

outgoing, friendly
loud, boastful, rude
informal
immature
hardworking
think they have all the answers
extravagant
wasteful
lacking class consciousness
disrespectful of authority
racially prejudiced
ignorant of other countries
wealthy
generous
always in a hurry
prudish
think they should be the authority on world affairs

Obviously in both lists, American and Dutch, these traits or qualities may or may not be true of individuals. Part of the value of an overseas experience is learning how to get to know others as they are and not as you think they are.

KNOWLEDGE OF OURSELVES

We will never get to know **everything** about another person or culture nor, indeed, about ourselves or our own culture. The famous "Johari Window" shows how people are known and unknown to themselves and others.[8]

	Known to Others	Unknown to Others
Known to Self	Known/Open	Hidden
Unknown to Self	Blind	Great Unknown

The **known** or open aspects of ourselves are comprised of those personality traits, talents, etc., of which both we and others are aware, for example, our teaching ability, our singing voice, or our sense of humor. These fall within the known area of our total person.

Then there are traits, talents, and qualities which we know about ourselves, but which others do not know. Others may not know that you have always wanted to be a gymnast or that you have a deep desire to be liked by others. These facts or qualities which you alone know but do not reveal to others are within the **hidden** area of your total person.

There is yet another area of ourselves which others perceive but of which we ourselves are unaware. This is the **blind** area. I have a friend, for example, who has a beautiful gift of drawing each person in a group into the conversation. If a newcomer is present, she is able to draw connections between that person and the others which give the entire group a point of contact. The gracious manner in which she does this has the effect of immediately including the newcomer in the group. One day I commented to my friend how much I admired and appreciated this ability of hers. She was amazed because she was totally unaware of it.

The last area of knowledge is the **great unknown** of which both we and others are unaware. This area constitutes a domain of discovery which makes life an adventure.

One of the benefits of having friends who will be honest enough to share their perceptions of us *with* us is that we can grow in awareness. We may not always like what we learn, but without their valuable feedback, we remain unaware of an important aspect of ourselves. If it is a negative trait, once it is known to us, we may be able to change it; on the other hand, we may need to claim a positive quality that we have not recognized. I have been grateful to those friends who have made me aware of negative traits which were impeding my relationships with others. I have been equally grateful for those friends who have helped me become aware of positive qualities of which I had not been conscious. A recent experience stands out in my mind. When applying for a new position, I had asked several people who knew me rather well to write recommendations for me. One person sent me a copy of his recommendation. I was stunned by his perceptions of strengths I had been totally unaware of. It was so encouraging that I pasted the paper up where I could see it and *remember* to be the person he had seen in me. Feedback, whether positive or negative, enables us to grow and develop to our fullest capacity.

Just as individuals can be looked at in terms of the known and unknown, so can countries and cultures. Our actions and reactions in cross-cultural situations are often based on what we don't know about our own culture as much as what we don't know about the host culture. It is helpful to be aware of our preconceptions, ready to admit they may be erroneous, and equally ready to change them. We must also be open to exploring our own culture so we understand our own cultural conditioning and how it is demonstrated in our behavior.

CROSS-CULTURAL ADAPTATION

Let's take a look at the actual process of culture shock or cultural adaptation in terms of some common developmental stages.[9]

1. Entry, fascination, excitement
2. Subtle irritation
3. Complete frustration, depression
4. Coping
5. Belonging to the country

Phase One—Entry/Fascination

The first phase of cultural adaptation has been termed the *entry/fascination stage* or *honeymoon* phase. It encompasses the initial excitement preceding the move and can last up to six months after the actual move. But it is important to realize that individual time cycles in undergoing this experience vary greatly; be sensitive to your own. For you, this excitement phase could last two months, or, as one person declared, "I **never** experienced it!" This period is one of delighted discovery as you notice everything that is new, different, and interesting. During this period you will probably hear yourself and others expressing your reactions with such words as *cute, quaint, charming.*

One of the differences we noticed and found captivating in The Netherlands was the omnipresence of flowers—flower boxes everywhere, flower pots on window sills, flower stalls, flowers on the backs of bicycles, even houseboats complete with lace curtains and flowers. Another sight new to us was a pasture on our suburban street where contented cows grazed. Occasionally, they wandered into the road, undeterred by cars attempting to pass. The first time a cow wandered into the path of our car I called the Dutch police because I was sure someone would hit the cow or the cow would wander away. The policeman was not at all surprised. He informed me that cows wandered onto the road all the time but that they seldom got hurt. We were also acutely aware of the millions of bicycles Dutch citizens use as a primary form of transportation. To facilitate the traffic flow there were separate bicycle lanes or paths throughout the country. I now miss that convenient and safe division of traffic when I bicycle in the U.S.

At the end of the chapter there is a space for you to list those noticeable differences you enjoyed when you first arrived in your host country. You may also correct previous misconceptions. One young mother I met, for instance, was pleased to discover that The Netherlands is one of the few European countries where she could buy peanut butter for her children's peanut butter and jelly sandwiches.

Two groups working through the entry stage made up lists of their likes and dislikes about The Netherlands. One list is from adults; the other is from a group of sixth-grade American boys, students at the American School of The Hague.

What I Like about Living in The Netherlands

Boys' List	*Adults' List*
school	flowers
school swimming pool	museums
school art center	proximity to other countries
school computers	travel opportunities
school ski trip	opportunity to learn new
school field trips to other	language
countries	public transportation
school buses (yeah!*)	public safety
American baseball	ability to walk safely at night
church	bicycle paths
travel	fresh vegetables, eggs, etc.
parks and forests	open air markets
	famous works of art,
	historical sites

(*they were comfortable tour buses)

It is interesting to observe that most of the items on the boys' list are rooted in the American community and the American school in The Hague, which reflect the boundaries of their world. The adults are more aware of the attributes of the new country.

Phase Two—Subtle Irritations

Just as a marital honeymoon gives way to other phases, so does the cultural honeymoon. As your personal experiences begin to influence some of your initial responses, subtle irritations and frustrations usher in a second phase in which you become aware of the difficulties of living abroad and the aspects of living in your new environment that you don't like. This phase normally lasts six to eight months, but, unfortunately, it tends to repeat itself a second or even a third time after you have successfully engineered your way through it and have gone on to the coping, adapting, and belonging phases. For me, the small narrow Dutch streets I first called "quaint" and "charming" became a source of frustration when I discovered it was common practice for delivery trucks to double park without paying any attention at all to the growing line of cars behind them. Boxed in by traffic on both sides, I often sat for half an hour—where could I go? Into the canal was the only choice! As a result I was late for more than one appointment. Parking spots were at a premium in this small country, and I often had to search for one blocks away from my destination. Another disconcerting traffic rule is that all drivers on the right have the right of way. This was difficult to get used to because it included drivers emerging from tiny alleys on to main thoroughfares—and they wouldn't stop but would come out at full speed.

A primary difference to deal with is, of course, the language. Perhaps one of the greatest frustrations in The Netherlands comes when you try to speak Dutch only to find the Dutch speaking to you in English. The result is, of course, that you end up speaking English most of the time because it is easier—and you feel deprived of the opportunity to develop your proficiency in Dutch. That had happened to me as an AFS exchange student in Luxembourg—I had acquiesced to my host family's desire to practice their English (which meant my French never improved). So, in The Netherlands I refused to speak English and persisted in speaking Dutch (and did the same in Denmark with Danish). Sometimes it seemed like a contest between me and the shopkeepers. To my inquiry in Dutch, they would reply in English, to which I would reply in Dutch. Back and forth we would go in separate languages until through my sheer persistence the conversation continued in Dutch. I think they were motivated by a desire to be considerate, and they really didn't expect an American to speak their language. It took this kind of dogged effort, but I became fluent in both Dutch and Danish.

Because English is so widely spoken, it is easy to fall prey to the temptation not to learn the host language at all, limiting your ability to communicate and interact with people in the host culture. As time goes on, the resulting isolation aggravates the problems encountered in the adaptation process.

Phase Three—Frustration/Culture Shock

Then there comes a day when the frustrations of continuously trying to adjust to so much that is new catch up with you, and you hit rock bottom, plagued by feelings of helplessness and despair. You feel victimized (after all, aren't all these inconveniences the result of ill will directed at **you** personally?) and depressed, and you wonder why you came here in the first place. This can result in your directing a lot of anger towards your husband, his company, God, etc. Now is the time to make a list of all those features of the host country that you don't like, just as you did for your "likes." It will be easy, I can assure you. Again, there is space provided for you at the end of the chapter. Following is another sample list from adults and children living in The Netherlands:

What I Don't Like about Living in The Netherlands

Boys' List	*Adults' List*
distance away from friends living in the same city	traffic
	language
"weird" Dutch food	distance from family and friends at home
can't get favorite American foods	long lines in markets and banks
Dutch kids tease you, attack you, are anti-American	smaller houses
fewer conveniences	lack of American sports
	lack of opportunity for wife to work or study

Now, make your own list of dislikes and then compare it with your list of likes. When you have hit bottom, you should be able to remember the things you like even though they are presently overshadowed by feelings of frustration and anger. Try this exercise of listing both your likes and dislikes in your host country with a group of people who have been there for varying lengths of time. It will be encouraging to realize that someone else has survived this stage of adaptation, and you might also find that your likes outnumber your dislikes.

In this third stage you are out of balance. Coping skills acquired at home or in another culture are inadequate to meet the demands of the new situation. The uncertainties and fears that result from this disorientation can cause various reactions.

Fight. Some people fight their circumstances and/or the host culture, the company that sent them, the spouse who accepted the assignment (most moves occur when husbands change jobs, but with the increasing number of women with careers, this is changing), or God, who should know what they are going through and be in better control of the situation.

Flight. Some people go home for extended visits during this period, which may only postpone coming to grips with the problem. Others just leave, abandoning their spouse in the process—which usually leads to divorce. Those who flee frequently leave behind shocked friends and acquaintances who either weren't aware of the severity of the person's problems or simply didn't know what to do. Even pastors often feel helpless when they encounter a wife in an extreme state of culture shock. They do not know how to help, and they may be experiencing their own culture shock. Church structures rarely provide opportunities to discuss the issue in groups, and ministers have expressed hesitation to get involved on an individual basis with someone in a state of relatively severe depression. They know that they may have insufficient training for this kind of counseling. While severely depressed persons should seek help from professional counselors, this book provides guidelines for the conduct of workshops and small group discussion that can benefit almost anyone going through the stresses of cross-cultural adaptation. Beyond simply sharing tea and sympathy, participants can develop new friendships while expanding their own abilities to cope and flourish in a new environment.

Withdrawal (a less severe form of the flight reaction). Some people tend to stay home alone or to see only a very few friends; there is a reluctance to get involved, to take responsibility or make decisions. In the work place the two symptoms most commonly encountered are avoidance of decision making and failure to accept responsibility.

Even your body joins in by reacting with a number of physical symptoms which mask the underlying feelings actually responsible for your discomfort. Physical complaints can often be a message from your body to pay attention to your emotional and psychological needs. Some of the symptoms experienced by persons during this phase include constant minor aches, pains, or illnesses; sleeplessness or sleeping too much; compulsive eating or extreme weight loss.

It is paradoxical that just when you need the companionship, reinforcement, and support of your friends the most, you feel impelled to withdraw and cut off contact, to retreat into your shell with your physical and psychological ailments.

Thomas Holmes and Richard H. Raye, two psychologists who are considered experts in helping individuals identify and deal with stress, devised the Social Readjustment Rating Scale, which assigns different values to particular changes and events depending on their severity or stress quotient.[10] The idea is to identify those events you experienced during the past year, add the numerical value of each and then total your score. If you score two hundred or more, they advise you to take immediate action to reduce stress. Actually, if you were to add up only the normal changes entailed in an overseas move, without any additional stressful situations such as divorce, death, serious illness, or separation, the score comes close to three hundred. Now note the score resulting from the typical kinds of adjustments experienced by two study groups—443! Obviously, moving abroad produces a high level of stress in the individual.

Social Readjustment Rating Scale

The following is a typical score derived from the normal adjustments required in a cross-cultural move as experienced by respondents from two study groups.

Item No.	Item Value	Happened (X)	Your Score	Life Event
1.	100	____	____	Death of spouse
2.	73	____	____	Divorce
3.	65	____	____	Marital separation
4.	63	____	____	Jail term
5.	63			Death of close family member
6.	53	____	____	Personal injury or illness
7.	50	____	____	Marriage
8.	47	____	____	Fired at work
9.	45	____	____	Marital reconciliation
10.	45	____	____	Retirement
11.	44	____	____	Change in health of family member
12.	40	____	____	Pregnancy
13.	39	____	____	Sex difficulties
14.	39	____	____	Gain of a new family member
15.	39	x	39	Business readjustment
16.	39	x	38	Change in financial state
17.	37	____	____	Death of a close friend
18.	36	x	36	Change to different line of work
19.	35	____	____	Change in no. of arguments w/spouse
20.	31	____	____	Mortgage over $10,000
21.	30	____	____	Foreclosure of mortgage or loan

22.	29	x	29	Change in responsibili- ties at work
23.	29	___	___	Son or daughter leaving home
24.	29	x	29	Trouble with in-laws
25.	28	___	___	Outstanding personal achievement
26.	26	x	26	Spouse begins or ends work
27.	26	x	26	Begin or end school
28.	25	x	25	Change in living conditions
29.	24	x	24	Revision of personal habits
30.	23	___	___	Trouble with boss
31.	20	x	20	Change in work hours or conditions
32.	20	x	20	Change in residence
33.	20	x	20	Change in school
34.	19	x	19	Change in recreation
35.	19	x	19	Change in church activities
36.	18	x	18	Change in social activities
37.	17	___	___	Mortgage or loan less than $10,000
38.	16	___	___	Change in sleeping habits
39.	15	x	15	Change in no. of family gatherings
40.	15	x	15	Change in eating habits
41.	13	x	13	Vacation
42.	12	x	12	Christmas
43.	11	___	___	Minor violations of the law

443   Total score for 12 months

Phase Four—Coping

So how do you begin to cope? How do you regain some of the excitement, enthusiasm, and energy of the first phase of the curve? You usually come to the realization that you are truly dissatisfied with your life. You are not doing the things that you enjoyed at home, and you can't seem to figure out what you want to do now that you are abroad. It is difficult to initiate action when you are feeling inadequate and helpless. Feeling like a failure, you wonder, "What's happening to me? I never used to be like this. Am I out of my mind?" The confusion is compounded by feelings of guilt when you receive letters from home which are sprinkled with such phrases as, "You are so lucky! What a wonderful experience you all must be having." Your head tells you, "Yes, it is true. We are lucky," but inside you are asking yourself, "Why don't I feel lucky? Why am I so miserable?" and even more depressing, "What is wrong with me?"

To get through this phase, it is important to know and recognize that it is a perfectly normal part of the process. You are not alone. Perhaps if we were more open about our feelings, sharing them with one another would relieve much of the anxiety which results from thinking we need to keep them submerged and under control. Attempts to deny or control our gyrating emotions take an enormous amount of energy which could be harnessed for use in the adaptation process.

One way of taking charge is to set yourself some small manageable goals within a limited time period. Commit yourself to participate regularly in something you enjoy during the next month. Whether it is playing tennis weekly, joining the bridge group, enrolling in an art class, taking regular walks to explore your new city, or inviting a few couples over for dinner, do it *now*. Procrastination is a predominant characteristic of this phase.

Another good idea is to vow that at the next gathering you attend—whether a school PTA meeting or a worship service— you will make it a point to meet a new person or take steps to deepen your relationship with someone you already know. Invite that person to do something with you. She may need your invitation. Others are going through this experience too.

Indeed, when you have emerged victorious and feel at home, continue to reach out and help others. One effective way is to call and extend a specific invitation—"Let's play tennis tomorrow. I'll come by and pick you up at 2:00." Don't make it a vague, "Let's play tennis sometime." A person in this phase of culture shock may feel that vague invitations aren't really sincere, and when she hedges, the "proof" of that belief is that no one followed up on it. The extra reaching out may be just what the other person needs to be convinced that anyone cares about her. It may take five invitations, but be persistent. I remember the woman who invited me to play tennis and brushed aside my refusals. Wiser, or at least more experienced than I, she kept at me until I *did* play, and the event marked the beginning of a change in my attitude and ultimate recovery.

Be especially careful to watch family members for signs of culture shock. It is easy to write their actions off as simply irritating behavior. They may need help.

The coping phase starts when you begin to take steps toward functioning more fully within your new surroundings. Being more active in pursuing your personal interests will help, as will finding new interests.

Learn as much as you can about the people and culture around you. Reading about the country's history and customs, sharing in some of the national holiday festivities, learning the language, and developing relationships with your neighbors is a good way to get out of your shell. L. Robert Kohls in his excellent little book, *Survival Kit for Overseas Living*, provides a list of fifty questions (included at the end of this chapter) which if asked and answered about your host country will contribute significantly to the knowledge base needed for effective cross-cultural adaptation.

Also, participate in a newcomer orientation workshop if possible. The American Women's Club and some American churches in Europe have initiated programs attempting to address the problem of culture shock. The American Church in Paris has a well-organized program called "Bloom Where You Are Planted." Events are scheduled one day a week for four weeks in the fall. The programs are designed to help newcomers adjust to various aspects of life in Paris, ranging from using the metro system to shopping to finding an obstetrician. In the last few years, recognizing the need to deal with internal stresses, they have added presentations on cross-cultural adjustment.

Phase Five—Adaptation

Adapting to another culture involves learning both how to do things a new way and, even more important, knowing why they are done differently.

Behavior is an outgrowth of values, attitudes, knowledge, and the experiences and conditioning of one's culture. When you encounter people whose behavior is different from yours, the natural tendency is–assuming you don't like their behavior—to attribute it to bad manners or bad judgment, when in fact, it usually derives from different values or culturally determined customs. If you seek the logic behind the action, you may still not agree with it or even accept the reason, but it does become easier to understand.

I remember when it finally dawned on me that much of the Dutch behavior I didn't understand was the result of a large population living in a small area. The Netherlands is the most densely populated country in the world, and this affects people's ideas about how space should be used. Houses are generally much smaller than their American counterparts. The tiny kitchen and tiny appliances are **not** designed to frustrate the homemaker. They are designed to fit the space. The aggressive Dutch drivers, I believe, are simply asserting their right to a space of their own and have to compete for their place in the flow of traffic. Double-parking and blocking the road are accepted because it allows drivers to make deliveries and the like in a situation where there is no other choice.

It is a challenge to know how to function within a different cultural setting and still be yourself. It means learning all kinds of new habits—identifying yourself on the telephone by name instead of simply saying hello, shaking hands or kissing when you meet, taking flowers when you are invited to someone's home for dinner, waiting for the host to toast before you drink, etc. I remember my initial panic at an elegant dinner in Scandinavia. I'd never encountered five different types of glasses in one place setting before.

Remember the first time you stayed overnight with a friend's family, went away to college, or attended an embassy reception? Those were different culture groups too. You had to learn the rules. It is basically the same process but in a different country and with a new language. You've done it before; you can do it again.

Robert Kohls has developed a list of skills valuable for cross-cultural adaptation:[11]

tolerance for ambiguity	sense of humor
low goal/task orientation	warmth in human relationships
open-mindedness	self-reliance
strong sense of self	curiosity
nonjudgmentalness	perceptiveness
empathy	communicativeness
ability to fail	flexibility, adaptability
motivation	tolerance for differences

Based on your experience, which of these skills do you think he selected as the three most valuable in the adaptation process? His choices seemed strange at first because I would have chosen others; however, after reflection I agree with them.

1. Sense of humor
2. Low goal/task orientation
3. Ability to fail

A *sense of humor* is an absolute necessity (actually, I got this one right!). You need to be able to laugh at yourself and at the frustrations which beset you. However, I was surprised by the second item, *low goal/task orientation.* Kohls says that it is very important to be flexible and open to whatever you encounter; don't let yourself be so bound by an excessive concern for accomplishing a predetermined task in a predetermined way that you can't adapt to the realities of your new situation. His emphasis on the *ability to fail* also surprised me, but it is so true. The value of this came home to me on more than one occasion. Failure is inevitable in a new country where so much is strange and unfamiliar.

Vicky Baker, an American in The Netherlands, interviewed several fellow Americans living in The Hague and came up with a typology for people who live abroad.[12] These types relate closely to the processes I have been discussing here.

Encapsulators. These are the people who participate exclusively in their foreign or American community, make little or no effort to learn the local language, and have little contact with local people. These people are akin to those who fight, flee or withdraw, as discussed above. But instead, they simply create a world of their own, which they inhabit almost as if the host country doesn't exist.

World Citizens. These people are comfortable in both their own communities and in the new society. They develop at least some modest skill in the local language, and they get involved in activities with local people. These are people who learn about and derive benefits from living in a foreign culture.

Bicultural. These people integrate into the new culture, master the language, and have many social contacts in the native society. These are the integrators.

Most people who are successful at living overseas *adapt.* They maintain their primary identity in and with their own culture, but they also reach out, make contact with the host culture, and learn both to accept the differences encountered and to function effectively within them.

Integrating into another culture is difficult. It requires a high degree of commitment and perseverance, along with strong language learning skills and the ability to split your cultural identity without negative psychological consequences.

In the end, the most important thing to remember is that you are *you!* There is no one else exactly like you. Down to your fingerprints you are the unique person God created you to be.

Something that has been most helpful to me and others in revealing the skills and abilities we already have and which can help us in new situations is the Life Satisfaction Exercise (see page 48). This exercise involves preparing a time line of your life from birth to the present, charting the low moments and high moments you have experienced and the skills you have developed in dealing with them. You will be amazed at what you learn about yourself and the degree to which your past experience applies to or constitutes a resource for the present. Even more startling is the realization that unless the skills involved were physical and have changed through aging or disability, you still have them; all those skills, abilities, and qualities which you used then are available to you now. They are God's gifts to you in this process of growth. How can you use them now?

Let me stress again how valuable this particular exercise has been to persons in new situations, and I encourage you to use it by yourself or in a group.

If you begin to feel comfortable enough to relax, branch out, and expand your horizons, you will find your life greatly enriched, so much so, in fact, that you will never be the same again. You may even find yourself adapting to new ideas and doing things you would never have thought of before. The promise of the prophet Isaiah which applied to my very first move still continues to be true: "Do not cling to events of the past or dwell on what happened long ago. Watch for the new thing I am going to do. It is happening already. You can see it now" (Isaiah 43:18-19). The freedom to be yourself, aware that you will experience fear, difficulty, disappointment, and problems along the way, in addition to joy and pleasure, releases you to be a whole person in relation to others. Just asking for help from a resident of the country (as occurs in some of the biblical stories included at the end of the chapter) may lead to satisfying friendships. People like to know they have something to offer, and often nationals of other countries think we Americans don't need them—we somehow appear to "have and know it all."

CROSS-CULTURAL BIBLICAL EXPERIENCES

In Egypt, Reverend David Johnson of the Maaidi Community Church has for a number of years offered two annual all-day retreats for women to discuss the subject of women in exile. Here are some of the questions he poses for discussion at the retreats. I find them inspirational in the degree to which they draw one into a deep and meaningful consideration of the experience of separation which is part of living abroad.

1. How do you (or did you) handle some of the various symptoms of exile? Are you at home here now?
2. What other life experiences remind you of exile?
3. Do you understand exile to be something bad, something good, something potentially bad, or something potentially good?
4. As you read the Bible and meet its people, do you find it possible to take their stories and relate them to your own life? Or is it too much of another world, another God, another kind of experience from your own?
5. What things about the story of Sarah make you feel better? What makes you feel worse about her story?
6. Discuss the statement, "God has a history of working best with God's people while in exile."
7. Is there a sense of "call" to your presence (and your spouse's) in Egypt? How do you articulate and share that—with each other and with others?

These questions guided my thinking about three biblical stories which involve encounters between natives and foreigners—"The Samaritan Woman at the Well," "The Canaanite Woman," and "The Widow and Elijah." At the end of the chapter I have cited these stories and listed some questions to stimulate thought and discussion. It is interesting to note comparisons between the biblical stories and our own contemporary experiences, and you may wish to use some of them as a basis for small group discussions.

As you prepare for and then experience this time of adjusting to a new culture, some of the most meaningful and helpful guidance can come from looking at the lives of people in the Bible—those people whose stories are our stories. They too felt fears and doubts and experienced dislocation; yet it is apparent that God often works with chosen people most effectively by calling them away from their surroundings. Could it be that God needs to get our attention through the difficulties and hardships of isolation and transplantation which strengthen and purify us? As normal supportive systems are removed, we are forced to seek God's presence in the new and unfamiliar situations.

Think of some of those persons God set apart through geographical dislocation: Abraham and Sarah, Lot and his family, Moses and Aaron, Joseph, the children of Israel taken into captivity in Babylon, and Ruth. In the New Testament we read of Priscilla and Aquila moving often from place to place, of Paul who was called out from his own people in a dramatic and isolating experience.

Read the story of Abraham and Sarah in Genesis 12-22. They lived comfortably established in the country of their fathers when one day Abraham received a command from God (Genesis 12:1): "Go from your country and your kindred and your father's house to the land that I will show you." Abraham obeyed God immediately, it says. From this response, what kind of relationship do you imagine Abraham and God had? How would Abraham know it was God speaking and not just his imagination? How would Sarah also be convinced this was God's plan? If we were to put this in today's setting, what means would God use to call you forth to a new country? How do you think God may be involved in your move? If you role-played Abraham, Sarah, their children and their families in their response to the decision to move, who would be left behind? Using your own reactions as your guide, how do you think they would respond to each other? Would Sarah have considered or have wished to consider other options?

At the same time that God commanded Abraham to move out, God also promised him, "And I will make you a great nation and I will bless you and make your name great so that you will be a blessing" (Genesis 12:2). As Abraham and Sarah followed God's command, they experienced practical problems which they tried to solve themselves instead of seeking God's solutions. When a famine devastated the land, for example, they moved to Egypt instead of trusting God for help and guidance. Genesis 12:10-20 shows how God resolved some of the ensuing difficulties in which they became embroiled and which clearly stood in the way of the fulfillment of God's promise to Abraham.

As the years went by and Abraham and Sarah had no children and God's promise did not seem humanly possible, they began to wonder what God could mean. Doesn't this all sound only too familiar when we try to figure out how God's purposes will be accomplished? Abraham and Sarah thought perhaps the son of Abraham's slave, Eleazar, would be the source of fulfillment of the promise (Genesis 15:3), but that was not to be. Then Sarah tried to suggest that Abraham have a son by her slave Hagar (Genesis 16:1-3). All their attempts to make God's promise come true through their own efforts only resulted in problems and delayed the unfolding of God's plan. Only when things looked completely impossible did God bring them a son, Isaac. It seems that Isaac's birth was a turning point for Abraham and Sarah's own trust and faith. Abraham's trust in God grew so that he was even willing to sacrifice his only son if this was God's will (Genesis 22:1-18). Through Abraham's total commitment, God was able to bring forth the plan for the people. "Abraham believed God, and it was reckoned to him as righteousness, and he was called the friend of God" (James 2:23).

How can you compare Abraham and Sarah's experience to your own? What promise could God be bringing to fruition through this experience? In what ways have you grown that you would not have if you had remained where you were?

Ruth was another person removed from her own country, but by her own choice. The small book of Ruth tells the story of a foreigner, a young Moabite woman, who married one of the two sons of Naomi, a Jew. After the deaths of Naomi's husband and both sons, Naomi became embittered and decided to return to her home town of Bethlehem (because she had heard that God had visited it). Naomi and her two daughters-in-law were at a crossroads. Naomi urged them both to go back to their own families; she had no more sons to marry, no opportunity for their future. Orpha listened to Naomi and returned to her home. Ruth, however, chose to stay with Naomi. This decision seems remarkable to me. In Old Testament times widows had no status, no rights, and their futures were bleak. Furthermore, Moabites were hated by Jews. Yet, out of a love which transcended custom, Ruth chose to go with Naomi. "Where you go, I will go, and where you lodge I will lodge; Your people shall be my people, and your God my God; Where you die I will die, and there will I be buried." (Ruth 1:16-17). She chose not only Naomi and her people but also the God of Judah.

When we moved to The Netherlands, I thought often of Ruth's choice. It is hard to imagine making a choice so contrary to common sense and custom. Through her incredible love and selfless devotion Ruth became a member of one of Israel's most respected families and in the lineage of Jesus Christ. How does Ruth's life have significance or relevance to yours?

Another biblical story of life in a foreign country is that of Joseph, who was sold into slavery by his brothers and sent out of his native land. How did this seemingly evil situation become God's plan? Through the skillful management of responsibilities entrusted to him as a slave to Potiphar, Joseph quickly rose to a high position, but he never forgot the God of Israel. He never substituted wealth or power for honor and worship of God alone. His story includes further injustice when Potiphar's wife had him imprisoned because her desires were thwarted by Joseph's faithfulness to the laws of his God. Imprisoned and seemingly alone and forsaken, Joseph listened to the dreams God provided, which proved to be the very means for his freedom and future success. He was freed and became second in power only to the pharaoh. Through his success his family and the lineage of Israel were ensured. Long in advance God had prepared a man who would provide for God's own people to be saved from the disaster of famine that threatened to extinguish them. What appeared to be totally negative became a means of life (Genesis 37-50). Does your own exile have any elements similar to Joseph's story?

It has been said that to "hang in there" is a definition of faith. None of us is perfect. Each of us is human and, like Abraham and Sarah, we often grow in faith and trust through our own defeats, failures, and denials. Even Peter, one of Jesus' closest friends, denied him three times and ran away like a coward. Jesus promised us that we did not chose him. He chose us (John 15:16). God continues to reach out to us, to be revealed to us, to keep promises to us in spite of ourselves. Do not be afraid but honor God, who knows your every need and who will provide.

EXERCISES

Exercise 1: Likes and Dislikes

What I Like about This Country

_____   _____

_____   _____

_____   _____

_____   _____

What I Don't Like about This Country

_____   _____

_____   _____

_____   _____

_____   _____

Exercise 2: Three Biblical Stories

Read three stories:

1. The Samaritan Woman at the Well—John 4:7-42.
2. The Canaanite Woman—Matthew 15:21-28.
3. The Widow and Elijah—1 Kings 17:8-24.

All three stories describe an encounter between a native and a foreigner: two of them with Jesus as the foreigner, and one with Elijah in that role.

1. What needs are expressed in the stories? How was a foreigner able to fulfill the needs of the native? How was the native able to fulfill the needs of the foreigner? What qualities were called for?
2. How can you overcome the feeling of being a foreigner? How can you cross the cultural boundaries? What qualities are necessary in order to overcome the "them" and "us" syndrome?
3. Read Acts 11:5-17. How do your own prejudices stand in God's way?

4.   In what ways can we reduce the differences between "them" and "us" and increase interdependence? How can you **personally** do so?

Exercise 3: Life Satisfaction Exercise[13]

Record the major events and important times in your life on the grid below. The horizontal axis represents age intervals; the vertical represents degree of satisfaction.

1.   Place a dot(s) within each age interval at the level of satisfaction or dissatisfaction associated with the event/time.
2.   Write a one-word descriptor for each dot that identifies the event/time represented by the dot.
3.   Join the dots to indicate general patterns of life satisfaction.

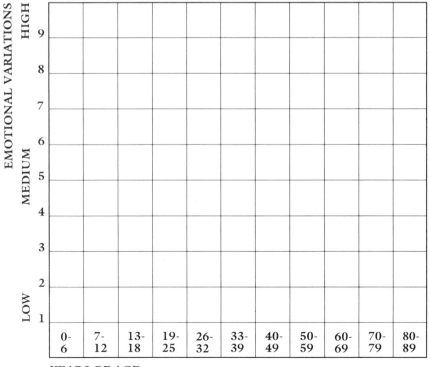

The following example represents my own life experience:

1. teaching Sunday school
2. marriage
3. divorce
4. college
5. marriage
6. children/family
7. seminary

8. article on travel, writing
9. Europe
10. Holland
11. Bible Club
12. book
13. church
14. training at Blanton-Peale

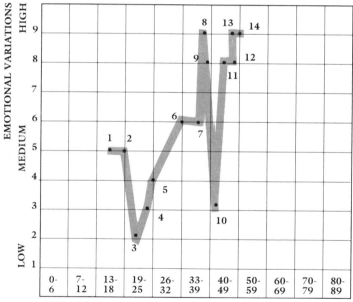

After completing the grid, take some time to think about the following questions. You may want to write down some of your thoughts. Then choose at least a few of the questions to discuss with a partner or small group.

1. What made your most satisfying points satisfying?
2. What made your least satisfying points unsatisfying?
3. Think of several times in your life when you were powerful (using your full potential) versus powerless (blocked from your inner strength, resources) and identify what or who empowered you.
4. What were you doing at the time of your life when you considered yourself most/least successful?
5. What/who has facilitated your growth?
6. What have you had to let go of to support your growth?
7. How can you apply what you have learned in the past to your present situation?

Exercise 4: Fifty Questions

Here are fifty basic questions about your host country and culture. They are not intended to constitute an inclusive list. Many more will be suggested as you attempt to answer these. Nevertheless, when you have the answers to the following fifty, you may consider yourself well beyond the beginner stage.

Go through the list now and write down the answers to as many as you can. Return to the list periodically, both as a guide and as a check on the progress of your quest for information.

1. How many people who are prominent in the affairs (politics, athletics, religion, the arts, etc.) of your host country can you name?
2. Who are the country's national heroes and heroines?
3. Can you recognize the national anthem?
4. Are other languages spoken besides the dominant language? What are the social and political implications of language usage?

5. What is the predominant religion? Is it a state religion? Have you read any of its sacred writings?
6. What are the most important religious observances and ceremonies? How regularly do people participate in them?
7. How do members of the predominant religion feel about other religions?
8. What are the most common forms of marriage ceremonies and celebrations?
9. What is the attitude toward divorce, extramarital relations, plural marriage?
10. What is the attitude toward gambling?
11. What is the attitude toward drinking?
12. Is the price asked for merchandise fixed or are customers expected to bargain? How is the bargaining conducted?
13. If, as a customer, you touch or handle merchandise for sale, will the storekeeper think you are knowledgeable, inconsiderate, within your rights, completely outside your rights?
14. How do people organize their daily activities? What is the normal meal schedule? Is there a daytime rest period? What is the customary time for visiting friends?
15. What foods are most popular and how are they prepared?
16. What things are taboo in this society?
17. What is the usual dress for women and men? Are slacks or shorts worn? If so, on what occasions? Do teenagers wear jeans?
18. Do hairdressers use techniques similar to those used by hairdressers in the United States? How much time do you need to allow for an appointment at the hairdresser?
19. What are the special privileges of age and/or sex?
20. If you are invited to dinner, should you arrive early, on time or late? If late, how late?

21. On what occasions would you present (or accept) gifts from people in the country? What kinds of gifts would you exchange?

22. Do some flowers have a particular significance?

23. How do people greet one another? Do they shake hands, embrace, or kiss? How do they leave one another? What does any variation from the usual greeting or leave-taking signify?

24. If you are invited to a cocktail party, whom would you expect to find among the guests: foreign business people, men only, men and women, local business people, local politicians, national politicians, politicians' spouses, teachers or professors, bankers, doctors, lawyers, intellectuals such as writers, composers, poets, philosophers, religious clerics, members of the host's family (including in-laws), movie stars, ambassadors or consular officials from other countries?

25. What are the important holidays? How is each observed?

26. What are the favorite leisure and recreational activities of adults, of teenagers?

27. What sports are popular?

28. What kinds of television programs are shown? What social purposes do they serve?

29. What is the normal work schedule? How does it accommodate environmental or other conditions?

30. How will your financial position and living conditions compare with those of the majority of people living in this country?

31. What games do children play? Where do children congregate?

32. How are children disciplined at home?

33. Are children usually present at social or ceremonial occasions? If they are not present, how are they cared for in the absence of their parents?

34. How does this society observe children's "coming of age"?

35. What kind of local public transportation is available? Do all classes of people use it?
36. Who has the right of way in traffic: vehicles, animals, pedestrians?
37. Is military training compulsory?
38. Are the largest circulation newspapers generally friendly in their attitude toward the United States?
39. What is the history of the relationship between this country and the United States?
40. How many people have emigrated from this country to the United States or other countries? Are many doing so at present?
41. Are there many American expatriates living in this country?
42. What kinds of options do foreigners have in choosing a place to live?
43. What kinds of health services are available? Where are they located?
44. What are the common home remedies for minor ailments? Where can medicines be purchased?
45. Is education free or compulsory?
46. In schools are children segregated by race, caste, class, or sex?
47. What kinds of schools are considered best: public, private, parochial?
48. In school, how important is learning by rote?
49. How are children disciplined in school?
50. Where are the important universities of the country? If university education is sought abroad, to what countries and universities do students go?

Reprinted with permission from L. Robert Kohls, *Survival Kit for Overseas Living*, pp. 46-49. Adapted from a list developed by Joan Wilson, Foreign Service Institute, U.S. Department of State. Another guide to what questions to ask when learning about another country and culture "on site" is *Transcultural Study Guide*. (see bibliography).

four

Who Are You?

TAKING STOCK

A major move and the breaking of old ties offers the chance for "time out" to stop, think, and take stock of our lives—if we choose to do so. It is easy to become so enmeshed in activities and everyday needs that we rarely allow ourselves this luxury. Moving at least provides a change in our schedules and an opportunity to reflect on who we are and where we are going, but even overseas the "have to's" of today can often preempt the long-range planning toward tomorrow.

Taking stock is a process only you can do for yourself. After the essentials have been unpacked, living space organized, the kids settled in school, shopping and the money system decoded, and a routine developed, you begin wondering what to do next.

A statement I hear often from women in culture shock is, "You have to keep busy here." When I ask why, the usual response is, "So that you won't think about it." *It* seems to mean both being here and not being wherever you came from, which includes missing the relationships and activities that formed a large part of your life and identity. The absence of these connections and of close friends and family are part of what you "don't want to think about."

MEETING GOD

Escaping into busyness prevents us from reflecting on what is happening to us and from confronting the situation as it is or taking the action we need to take. It may even be a way of preventing an encounter with God. Just as God met Elijah in the wilderness under the broom tree (1 Kings 19:1-18), God will meet us in our wilderness. If we escape into preoccupation with many things, we may miss God's gracious provision for us there. Elijah was discouraged and afraid, and so he fled into the desert; but God provided the nourishment he needed to reach Mt. Sinai, God's holy mountain, where God was revealed in a new way and provided Elijah with new direction. Like Elijah, you and I are not bound by the way in which God apprehended us yesterday. We must be open to God's new revelation to us today.

If we will withdraw to God and listen, we may discover we have been given a precious gift of time in which to reevaluate who we are, what we want to do with our lives, how we can more fully live up to God's vision. Here is an opportunity to explore a change in direction, try out new things, or use new and broadening experiences to develop and enrich our present direction.

DEFINING WHO YOU ARE

Have you, for example, ever sat down and tried to define who you are? Time and time again as we modern nomads move around the world, we are asked to introduce ourselves. Even if we have lived in the same town twenty years, we are asked to introduce ourselves as we join new groups or meet new people. I have listened more times than I can count to what seems to be the standard introduction for a woman: "My name is ———. We moved here from ——— and we're going to be here ——— months/years. We have ——— children at the ——— school. My husband works for ———."

If Shakespeare's line, "All the world's a stage, and all the men and women merely players," is accurate, what real identity lies behind the roles being played in your drama? What makes you the *unique* person God created you to be?

For example, to find the essence of who I am, I needed to peel away the different layers of my identity, like peeling away the layers of an onion. My name is Gretchen Janssen. My given name, Gretchen (a source of much pain to me as I grew up and found only German shepherds or dachshunds named Gretchen), fits much better with my married name, Janssen, than it ever did with my maiden name, White. I always had a lot of conflicting feelings about my name because I knew I had been named after my very talented grandmother who had died when my mother was a small child. And I always thought "Marilyn" would be much more glamorous. As I've grown older, I've come to appreciate the uniqueness of my own name.

As I write this, I am forty-nine years old. I never thought age would make any difference and felt that I would be "as young as I feel," but I am finding age also defines a stage in one's life. The exciting discovery I am making is that the older I become, the more "me" I become.

I am a wife—to a man I love and respect, who is and has been a great influence in my life. We experience more enriching give-and-take now than we did earlier in our marriage, and I think it is partly because I am less reluctant, as I grow older, to disagree and fight for my own opinions. I am more attuned to my own thoughts and feelings, more free in expressing them, and as a result, give Jerry more of the gift of myself (even if he doesn't always like it.)

I am a mother with two sons, Andrew, twenty-one, and Matthew, nineteen. As I write this, Andrew has just graduated from Stanford University, an exciting time in his life. Matthew is coming into his own as a freshman at Washington University in St. Louis. Their growth adds great excitement to my life. I alternately rejoice as they amaze me with perceptive insights or with sensitivity or compassion for someone else and agonize with them as they meet difficulties or disappointments in their process of "becoming." Before they left home, I was often surprised at their insistence that we pray together before they went to bed, and I hope that their desire to share their daily life with God will continue and grow all their lives.

I am a Christian. More and more I believe the lifestyle modeled by Jesus Christ is the only one that makes any sense. It is a life in which God is honored as creator and parent of all and through which one seeks to love one's neighbor as oneself, which encompasses all Ten Commandments. For me it is best summed up in Romans 13:8-10:

> Owe no one anything except to love one another; for whoever loves his neighbor has fulfilled the law. The commandments, "You shall not commit adultery, You shall not kill, You shall not steal, You shall not covet" and any other commandment are summed up in this sentence, "You shall love your neighbor as yourself." Love does no wrong to a neighbor; therefore love is the fulfilling of the law.

Believing in Christ's way of life does not mean his example is always an easy one to follow. It often runs counter to my desires, but I believe it is the only fully human answer to living in an interdependent world. Some of my greatest joy comes in sharing important moments and events with my friends— whether it is sharing joy or sharing pain and struggle. It is exciting to pray for and with each other and marvelous to see God working in and through our lives.

Why think about who you are? Because self-knowledge has a significant impact on how you adapt to new situations, such as living overseas. It affects your approach to and your perceptions of the challenges and opportunities and how you meet and grow in them.

At the same time, your identity is significantly affected by your move and by your new environment. Research has shown that loss of identity or the need to find new meaning in life is a major concern of women who move overseas. A second and related concern is developing meaningful relationships with others. Note that there is a reciprocity here since developing meaningful relationships (the key word, of course, is *meaningful*, which rarely results from frenetic activity designed to fill a void), requires some understanding of what is important to you (self-knowledge). At the same time, the development of meaningful relationships strengthens your sense of worth and makes you better able to ask the questions needed to lead you to self-knowledge.

Irrespective of where you live, there will always be a number of options available to you in meeting this challenge. You can embrace the situation, as one woman did, by stretching your arms wide and running forward shouting, "Paris, here I come!" Indeed, many rush into joining every group and club they hear about in order to meet people and throw themselves into the experience. Although you do need to meet people and begin building an identity in your new setting, frenetic activity, as we have noted before, is more often an escape from loneliness than a pursuit of significant involvement. It often ends in feeling obligated to activities and organizations you don't particularly enjoy.

Another way of reacting to the challenge is to go home, to flee (see my earlier discussion). Some people do. Some days I **wanted** to. Other people choose to live in their new location in body but continue to live mentally and emotionally in Texas or Massachusetts or wherever they lived before.

The option I have come to believe makes the most sense in the long run is to accept as a gift this opportunity to think through who you are. It will take time and involve thought, reflection, and some trial and error as you test your discoveries in your new environment, and it will take energy to both nurture yourself and share your gifts with others.

I'm learning it takes a balance. I need some friends with whom I can share my spiritual journey, with whom I can examine my experiences and try to make some sense out of them. What is the relationship of my life to God and how does God work in my life? These are people with whom I can be myself and share my joys and sorrows, my confusions, "my incoherent thoughts," as one friend says, without censure and with nonjudgmental acceptance. More than just a sympathetic ear, though, I need friends who will ask questions that will provoke me to think and grow.

I need mental stimulation, including conflict, that provokes me to wrestle with ideas and to stretch my brain. I need lots of physical stretching too, so I try to exercise—walk, swim and dance. I need time for hobbies, which for me are decorating, arranging flowers, listening to music, cooking or reading. I also need time to be with my family, time to enjoy a hobby or interest together, just having fun, but also time to be fully present to my husband and children to listen to them and pursue serious discussions.

Iraneus, an early Christian father, once said, "The glory of God is a human being fully alive." My own mental image of a fully alive human being is one who is being stretched in all directions. The obvious question is, of course, how to fulfill the potential God created in each of us. How can we become fully alive?

AN EXERCISE OF SELF-DEFINITION

So who are you? How do you define your uniqueness here and now? What makes you the never-to-be-repeated person you are? In Mark 5:1-20, Jesus asked the man, "What is your name?" "My name is Legion," he replied. "There are so many of us." Legion was a man tormented by many selves, fragmented and out of control. Like Legion, we have so many aspects of ourselves that we find it hard to sort them all out and weave them into a cohesive whole. To help in the process try the exercise entitled "Who Am I? Roles and Relationships."[14] Think of several adjectives that describe you. Think of words at both ends of the positive-negative spectrum, such as, enthusiastic, confused, caring, selfish, even-tempered, or depressed. Now think of as many ways as possible of introducing yourself through what is important to you. Usually these introductions are shaped by your roles or relationships—mother, wife, teacher, artist, etc. These aspects of our lives change with age, geographical location, state of mind, and current needs and interests. Match the adjectives to the roles and relationships you have listed to see which qualities and feelings you associate with each. Now rank the roles in order of importance to you. Which role is most meaningful to you now? Which could you give up most easily? Try to avoid ranking them the way you **should** feel. Be honest with yourself. Think about these roles and relationships and compare the way you spend your time with the way you have rank ordered them. Are you spending too much time on something which is less important to you than on something you value? Have these roles and relationships been changed by your move overseas or by new circumstances in your life during the last year?

Think about roles and relationships important to you but unavailable or missing where you live now. Is there something which suits your personality and fulfills your needs that can be a substitute? If, for example, you love being a grandparent and all your grandchildren are in the U.S., are there children in your neighborhood or circle of friends who are far away from their relatives and could be "adopted" for special activities? I know one friend who every so often has a cookie-baking day for all the small children she knows. They bake cookies, eat cookies (of course), and sing songs while she plays the guitar. A bachelor we know loved to bike and hike. He shared his interests with his scout troop and was the best scout leader our boys ever had. Part of his annual vacation was devoted to leading a group of scouts through the Swiss Alps on a rugged ten-day hiking trip. It was a trip one of our sons will never forget. He also used that opportunity to indulge in one of his favorite hobbies—photography—and has won awards for his photographs of that remote and beautiful wilderness area.

If you enjoy sports and can't play your particular favorite, is there a sport unique to your host country you can learn? It may mean that cross-country skiing or field hockey replaces basketball or golf. Or you may decide to organize American sports for your school or neighborhood. In The Hague several American families founded the American Baseball Foundation which sponsors baseball, soccer, and other sports for American children living in the area. A few enterprising fathers trained a soccer team to compete with Dutch teams—a real challenge because the Dutch are outstanding soccer players.

Legion, the man in the biblical story who was possessed by many selves, had been driven to the desert. When our many selves pull in different directions because we have not centered our lives and set our priorities, we too may feel fragmented and isolated. As you examine and assess the qualities which describe you and relate them to the roles and relationships which are important to you, you should be better able to define who you are and to discern for yourself what brings meaning to your life. Then you will be ready to ask how you can realistically be **more** yourself within the present situation. The question applies to all of us whether we are moving or not; but for those of us who **are** moving, the change can provide the opportunity to bring into focus issues which are central to our existence as human beings and as God's people.

EXERCISES

Exercise 1: Who Am I? Roles and Relationships

Adjectives that describe me:

      Positive   Negative

Roles and relationships that are important to me:

Now match the adjectives to the roles to see which qualities you bring to each role or relationship. Are you surprised by anything you have discovered?

Rank order the roles you have listed by importance to you. A helpful way to decide this is to consider which is most meaningful to you now and which you would give up most easily.

Have these roles and relationships been changed or affected by your move overseas or new circumstances in the last year? Do you spend more time on things less important than on other things you value more?

Share your discoveries with your small group.

Exercise 2: Milestones

With the help of drawings, this exercise helps you look back at major events or turning points in your life which have made you who you are today. Divide a piece of paper into six squares. Using a magic marker, draw (no artistic ability is necessary; stick figures are fine) six pictures that represent turning points or important milestones which changed the course of your life. Use different colors to express your feelings. When you have finished your drawings, discuss them with the group. This exercise, as simple as it sounds, can produce a deep exchange of experiences and bring you closer together both spiritually and emotionally with the others in the group.

To help you visualize how this exercise works, I have included one drawing (clearly **not** a masterpiece) of a turning point in my own life.

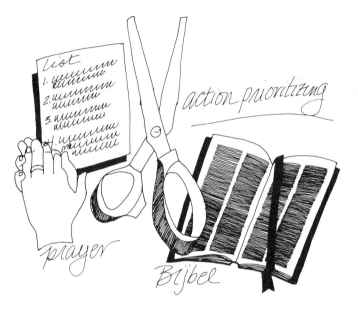

I began to think about who I was and what I wanted to do, and how this period fit into a larger plan for my life. I prayed and sought the scripture for God's will and word to me. I listed my activities and cut (note the scissors) out those things which did not promote my values and which used time and energy I needed for what I felt called to do. Taking this step was one of the most influential actions of my life. When I wrote the word *Bible*, you can see I wrote it in Dutch as I was speaking Dutch often with friends and neighbors.

five

Where Are You Going?

Having determined which roles and relationships are important to you, the next step is to determine your long-range goals and then choose short- and mid-range objectives which will lead to your ultimate destination. Ask yourself what you would like to be when you are eighty and what you would like to have done. Older people, looking back on their lives, too often express regrets about what they have not been or done. They are often aware of what they would do if "they could do it over again." I assume that you, as I, would prefer to arrive at old age with a sense of satisfaction with what you have done with your life. Take a few minutes, then, and write down in the space below your thoughts and responses to the following questions: When I am eighty years old, what kind of person do I hope to be? What do I hope to have been or to have done with my life? This will be your *life goal.*

This kind of long-range goal determines—or can determine—how you make all the little choices along the way. You won't always proceed on a straight, steady path, however. I have often felt as if I were taking two steps forward and six backwards, being led up blind alleys or around in circles. Sometimes I am sure that is exactly what has happened. I have also changed my life goal as I have grown and evolved. But no matter what mistakes you make, how many tangents you go off on, or how many times you miss your objective, you can always pick yourself up, learn from the experience, and go on. You may decide to continue as before; you may realize you need to make midcourse corrections or change direction entirely, but you can go forward with your life, perhaps strengthened and more aware of who you are than before.

In approaching this question of setting goals, both short- and long-term, the first step is to evaluate where you are now. You will then be in a better position to see how to move in the direction of your life goal. You must be in touch with your own needs in order to begin establishing your long-term goals; the exercise on roles and relationships in the previous chapter helped identify what is important to you. Let's now look at three areas of your life that are important components of who you are as a person: (1) relational (important family or other close relationships), (2) developmental (change and growth), and (3) personal (including physical and spiritual life). We'll talk about establishing goals later, but for the moment let's concentrate on these three areas of life.

RELATIONSHIPS

In a move abroad there is not only the opportunity for developing new kinds of relationships within your immediate (nuclear) family, but with your extended family as well. Often your own family will grow closer because you are braving a new world together. At the same time you may mourn the distance between yourself and parents, sisters and brothers, grown children or grandchildren. In all my conversations with women overseas, the distance from children who were living away from home, either attending college, working, or married with families of their own, was one of the most painful aspects of being abroad. Though less acute perhaps, the same applies to other family members or friends. For example, what do you do if someone becomes ill or an aging parent needs extra attention when you are living in another country. The short-term choices you make in dealing with these situations are related to your long-term vision of who you want to be and how you want to live your life. The amount of energy you choose to expend on relationships already important to you will affect the amount of energy you have available for forming new relationships in your current situation. You need also to choose the **kinds** of relationships you want to form and the **depth** to which you wish to develop them. If your existing relationships require most of your energy, you may experience conflict since one of the most enriching aspects of living abroad is developing relationships with people of the host country. You must examine these demands and opportunities in the light of your life goals.

SELF-DEVELOPMENT

Self-development can involve many different aspects of your life, from growth in your career and professional interests to education and travel and the acquisition of new skills. If you had to give up some important ambition or make a major personal or career sacrifice to accompany your husband and move your family to a new location, underlying feelings of frustration and restlessness may emerge when it comes to thinking of goals. You have already had to give yours up once! Yet, in my experience, it is just when the world seems to have closed in that unforeseen opportunities open up, opportunities for growth and development I would never have considered had I not encountered those closed doors. Within the reality of living in new situations, I have found unexpected and creative solutions to the problem of setting new goals for self-development. I believe such solutions are found by (1) carefully assessing your own needs, (2) weighing them thoughtfully against the circumstances in which you find yourself, and (3) matching your gifts and skills to the situation.

Where are you now physically? Do you want to improve your fitness or change some habits you don't like? Perhaps now is the time to do something about it! Living in a country where a large percentage of the population uses bicycles as a principal mode of transportation or walks instead of rides can be a great help in sloughing off some sedentary habits. If you know that you tend to weaken in such resolves, perhaps you can find a friend with whom you can establish a contract and to whom you can be accountable as you work toward your goal.

And what about your spiritual life? I have come to believe that change is God's gift to us in disguise. As painful as it can be, I believe God is reaching out to us to help us grow. Could God be reaching out to you? Perhaps you will want to check out the spiritual resources available to you; try going to worship or joining a group that is seeking spiritual direction. Listen for God's voice; it may be most insistent in a time of silence since we often hear God in ways we do not expect. Be attentive to the possibility of God's presence and look for God's guidance in setting goals for your life in your new environment.

MASLOW'S TRIANGLE

Another helpful way of getting a handle on goal setting is to study Abraham Maslow's hierarchy of values. Maslow, a well-known psychologist, developed a model called Maslow's Triangle, which depicts basic human needs in an ascending order. Maslow argues that each level of needs has to be met before the next in line can be attended to. The peak of the triangle represents a person utilizing his or her maximum potential.

Maslow reached his construct after extensively studying happy, healthy, and productive people, such as Franklin Roosevelt, Winston Churchill, Albert Schweitzer and others. He found that they had a number of common characteristics, such as a zest for life, the ability to find creative new solutions to old problems, a sense of humor, vigor, and the experience of peak states of being in which one feels wholly integrated. He also observed these same qualities in others who were living up to their full potential and whom he called self-actualized.

Maslow's theory is embodied in his hierarchy or triangle in which the needs at each level must be satisfied before the person can progress to the next higher level. The self-actualized person is the one who has met his or her needs at the first four levels and can now concentrate on doing that which realizes his or her full potential.

Dr. Thomas Gordon, in his discussion of Maslow, amusingly illustrates the theory with the example of a caveman (or cavewoman):

> Hungry (Level 1) caveman disregards Level 2 (Safety) and hunts dangerous game to get food. When Level 1 is satisfied, he takes care of Level 2 (Security) by stashing away rest of carcass in back of cave. What does he do then? Invites friends in for dinner—Level 3 (Social). Then for Level 4 he throws best party that forest ever saw (Accomplishment). If that works, he goes on to Level 5 (Self Actualization) by becoming a gourmet cookbook author—the wild Julia Child! [15]

Clearly, the different levels of need must be met in ascending order.

We can apply the same paradigm to setting priorities and goals based on knowing ourselves and assessing our current situation. It seems obvious to me how Maslow's ideas apply to a cross-cultural move. Level 1 (physical comfort) needs attention first and somewhat overlaps with level 2 (safety, security). The first step for you or any family moving abroad is to locate suitable living quarters which will meet your physical needs. At the same time that you seek the space that will accommodate you physically, you also need to pay attention to where you feel secure. Living conditions are different in various countries. This country's normal comfortable home may be a tent, but if you have been used to living in a high-rise apartment, you obviously have some adjusting to do.

The next step is to locate the food supply. Again, in a foreign country this can pose some problems. I can remember when I walked through a modern supermarket in Denmark for the first time. Canned peas and carrots could be identified by pictures on labels, but meat was, in the words of King Mongkutim in *The King and I*, "a puzzlement." The method of cutting meat was so different from what I was used to that our family ate only chopped meat for the first month until I learned what the other cuts were and how to prepare them.

Once you have settled into your living space and are familiar with your surroundings, you are ready for level 3 of Maslow's triangle. (Remember, just as in the cross-cultural adaptation process discussed on page 27, each person moves through these levels at an individual pace. Levels may also overlap.)

Now (level 3) is a good time to reread this book and intentionally decide how you will plan goals for your time in this new place. Belongingness is important. You can decide how you want to achieve it. You may wish to join groups available through your children's school, your husband's company, a church, the American Women's Club, or the embassy. You can also decide what kinds of relationships you want to develop. If you want to pursue in-depth friendships, you may choose to do the exercises in this book with a friend and share your discoveries.

One way we helped our children achieve a sense of belonging in our Danish neighborhood (and at the same time developed relationships with other parents) was to order a backyard playground set from the States. It was a heavy-duty wooden set which included two or three swings, a climbing area, and a slide. Although play sets are a rather common sight in yards in the U.S., no one had ever seen one at a private home in Denmark. It was a magnet for every child in the neighborhood and an immediate and spectacular success. The result? Our children made friends quickly and were easily assimilated into the neighborhood group. Consequently, they became fluent in Danish. We later learned from our neighbors that our children quickly became indistinguishable from theirs. Our only regret was leaving several disappointed families behind when we—and the set—moved to The Netherlands.

As you begin to decide where and with whom you wish to invest your energies and talents, you can set your own short-term achievement goals (level 4). Opportunities will present themselves, and you can decide which fit in with your long-term aims. For example, in The Netherlands as I began to know different people and share some of my ideas, I was asked to lead a workshop for women struggling with some of the issues involved in moving overseas. I was also asked to write a series of articles for the American Women's Club Magazine on the same subject, from a spiritual perspective. That was a challenge because they had published a similar series before, but it had been disappointing. I wanted to find an appropriate way to present my ideas yet be sensitive to other perspectives. The articles were well received and provoked much thought and discussion in the community. They also evolved into some of the core ideas for this book.

I suppose writing this book is an example of level 5, self-actualization (though it was not achieved while we lived overseas). Writing has become an important part of my life as I am asked to write for various publications and purposes. Anyone who loves what she (or he) is doing and lives up to full potential has reached level 5. It seems to me that we often fail to reach self-actualization by seeing circumstances, such as cross-cultural moves, as barriers instead of openings for getting in touch with latent hopes and dreams.

Try the Guided Imagination Exercise at the end of the chapter as a means of getting in touch with hopes and dreams that you may want to incorporate into your long-term goals.

VALUES AS REFLECTED IN GOALS AND CHOICES

During our two-year stay in Denmark, I encountered people I liked and respected whose values were very different from my own, and they made different choices from those I would have made in similar situations. I was forced to reassess my own values and found, as a result, that I began to make some different choices from those I would have made before. Some were enriching and helped me grow. Others were wrong for me. Sometimes I felt ridiculous, like the Man of La Mancha pursuing his impossible dream, because I was "out of sync" with the surrounding culture. Nevertheless, I learned to think through my choices and become more flexible but knew when it was important to make decisions that were different from those of the majority. Respect for other ways is essential, but

holding on to your values, and demonstrating them, is funda-
mental to your growth and well-being.

DETERMINING GOALS THROUGH PRAYER

One of the most important principles of goal setting is to
place your desires before God in prayer. Your direction may be
instantly clear to you, or it may come after a long time of
"waiting on the Lord."

Think of Queen Esther, who learned through her uncle
Mordecai of the plan to annihilate her people, the Jews. She told
him she could not enter the king's presence unless requested.
Mordecai's response speaks to us today:

> Think not that in the king's palace you will escape any more
> than all the other Jews. For if you keep silence at such a time
> as this, relief and deliverance will rise for the Jews from
> another quarter, but you and your father's house will
> perish. **And who knows whether you have not come to
> the kingdom for such a time as this?** Esther 4:13-14

Esther was in a position to take action that could make a
difference, but it involved the risk of disobeying a royal command. What was her reaction to this? She prayed and sought
God's guidance, asking Mordecai and all her people to fast and
pray with her before she took the action through which her
people were saved.

Another example is Nehemiah who presented the need to
rebuild the walls of Jerusalem to God in prayer before doing
anything about it. He was guided by God to present a plan to
the king who had the resources and the power Nehemiah lacked
to enable the rebuilding (Nehemiah 1-2).

In Psalms 25:12 we read, "Who is the person who fears the
Lord? That one will God instruct in the way God chooses." Lay
your goals in prayer before God. We have been promised that
if we seek God's direction, we will be guided and instructed.

A GOAL-SETTING PROCESS

I discovered that one of the best guides for helping me to set realistic goals was contained in Sandra Lanto's book mentioned earlier.[16] She describes a process (which is outlined here and which I have found enormously helpful in my own life) in which you keep your life goal in mind and then brainstorm goals in three areas of your life:

- Relational (any relationships you would like to have)
- Achievement (any or all creative or productive achievements you would like to make, without limitations)
- Personal (any enrichment or enjoyment you would like in your spiritual, emotional, physical or mental life)

(Note that Ms. Lanto's three areas for goal setting are slightly different from the three I suggest for the assessment of your present reality. I think of achievement goals as those that embody the concrete accomplishments you want to make in your own self-development.)

List as many goals in these areas as you can. Allow yourself five minutes for each list.

Relational	Achievement	Personal

Now select one goal from each area and circle it. Determine which of those three you wish to work on the most. That will be Goal A. The next most important will be Goal B, and the last will be Goal C.

Write the circled goals under each heading below and take five minutes to brainstorm activities that anyone who would want to achieve that goal might engage in; list them below the goal.

Relational   Achievement   Personal

Take a look at all the activities and cross off any for which the necessary resources (money, people or contacts needed, proper location, etc.) are unavailable to you or impossible to obtain. Then do the same for internal resources (courage, desire, etc.). Consider the activities that are left. Are you willing to spend at least one-half hour per week on them? If not, cross those off too. Number the ones remaining in the order they must be accomplished for you to attain your goal. Do this for all three goals.

The next step is to break these steps down month by month for the coming year. You may wish to make a block calendar, beginning next month. Be sure to note and block off time for things you have already planned, such as Christmas or vacations. You must be realistic in allocating the time you have available. Then make a complete list of the things you need to do next month to get started, regardless of time involved or sequence. Finally, block them in on the calendar in an orderly and manageable fashion.

In some months you will be able to take a number of small steps toward your goal. Other steps may take two, three, or even more months to accomplish. By breaking your goals into specific activities, time periods, and steps, you will be able to turn your choices from dreams to realities. Be flexible and realize it may take longer than you think, but you now have a logical plan of attack and are on the way instead of just wishing you were. You may also find that new activities come to mind or that new opportunities cause you to change direction. Plan after a time to reevaluate and, if desirable, redirect your efforts.

You should notice a natural progression from simpler activities to more complex ones, but an ordered progression which will enable you to accomplish what you desire. Writing a book was a long-term goal for me, preceded by several shorter-term goals, such as conducting a survey, developing and testing the material through workshops, evaluating attendees' reactions, and writing my thesis. As I write these words, I realize this book will soon be a reality and will mark the completion of a goal set eight years earlier. So congratulate yourself as you pass various markers along the way toward goal fulfillment.

We can claim the prayer in Colossians 1:9-12 to be a prayer for us as we seek to align our goals with God's will for our lives:

> For this reason we have always prayed for you, ever since we heard about you. We ask God to fill you with the knowledge of God's will, with all the wisdom and understanding that the Spirit gives. Then you will be able to live as the Lord wants and will always do what pleases God. Your lives will produce all kinds of good deeds, and you will grow in your knowledge of God. May you be made strong with all the strength which comes from God's glorious power, so that you may be able to endure everything with patience. And with joy give thanks to the Father, who has made you fit to have your share of what God has reserved for God's people in the kingdom of light. (Today's English Version)

The purpose of goal-setting efforts and of prayer is simply to enable us to lead a life worthy of God.

EXERCISES

Exercise 1: Guided Imagination

Begin by centering, which is accomplished as follows: Sit in a comfortable chair with your feet firmly on the floor, your eyes closed, and your body as fully relaxed as possible. Alternately tense and release your muscles. Breathe slowly and deeply from your abdomen. If you have distracting thoughts, firmly put them away and continue your rhythmic breathing for some minutes.

Now imagine a body of water. What kind of water is it, a natural body of water or artificial? Is the water still or running? Is it clear or muddy? Is it inside a building or outside? Is anyone with you? What are you doing? What is the other person, if there is one, doing or saying? Now look down into the water and let the images of things you have wanted to do, things you have desired and dreamed about, float up through the water—first things you dreamed about as a child, then as a teenager, then your dreams now.

Write down your dreams and what they tell you.

_____

_____

_____

_____

Now that you are in touch with some of your dreams, it is also time to understand how you have the power of choice. Make a list of all the *shoulds* you remember that have governed your life; for example, "I should always get the highest marks." A sign of a *should* is when you feel guilty because you will let someone down if you do not live up to one of these standards. List as many as you can.

_____

_____

_____

_____

Shoulds usually represent what others think you ought to do or be. Where did you hear yours? Are there some which are no longer relevant to your life or which you wish to discard? Cross them off the list. Now change the wording of those which remain so that *should* reads *I choose to.* By taking responsibility and exercising your power of choice, you free yourself from the *shoulds* which give others power over you. God has given us the freedom of choice. Without that freedom, we unconsciously conform to what others believe we should be, never able to choose on our own what is right for us, never needing to confess or repent when we choose wrongly, and never knowing the grace of God's forgiveness.

As you think about choices from this perspective, you may want to look at another exercise based on the story of Mary and Martha (Luke 10:38-42) which follows.

Exercise 2: Mary and Martha

An Exercise to Get in Touch with Two Sides of Ourselves—
I Should and *I Choose*

This exercise is for a group of four to twelve persons. It starts with one of the group members reading Luke 10:38-42 aloud. Then another member asks each of the questions listed below. The group answers spontaneously, letting as many answers emerge as possible and opening themselves to ideas they may not have thought of before. Ask everyone to imagine the text hovering in the center of the group and to attempt to encounter it on as many different levels as possible.

Questions
1. What do we already know about Mary and Martha from previous biblical study? (See John 11:1-45 and John 12:1-8)
2. What was Martha's concern?
3. Do you think Martha's attitude is influenced by the fact that the event occurred in her home?

4. What does her concern imply about her attitude toward herself, Jesus, Mary, or toward her responsibility? (On a flip chart or large piece of paper, ask the group to define the word *responsible*. What is responsibility? What does it mean to be responsible? Try to get as many different viewpoints as possible.)
5. How do you think Martha may have defined responsibility?
6. Does she have some needs of her own she may have been serving through her actions, and if so, what could they have been?
7. What do we know about Mary's decision?
8. What priorities does it reflect?
9. What may her needs have been?
10. How do you think she would define responsibility?
11. What does Jesus' response indicate about his feelings, his priorities?
12. How do you think he would define responsibility?
13. What are his attitudes towards both sisters?

Again, using guided imagination, set the scene. Imagine Mary sitting at Jesus' feet listening intently to all that he says. Imagine Martha coming in and complaining to Jesus. What does she say? How does Jesus react? Does Mary do anything or react in any way? What happens? Does Martha sit down too, or does she return to her chores? What does she say? What do Jesus and Mary do and say? With which person—Mary or Martha—do you identify?

All of us have both Mary and Martha within us. Using magic markers or crayons and a large sheet of paper, draw how you feel as Mary on half of the paper and how you feel as Martha on the other half of the paper. This exercise is **very** important. Do not skip it! As you draw, your hand will reveal truths the conscious part of your brain is unaware of. Use colors to indicate feelings and images and to draw the Mary and Martha parts of yourself. [17]

Exercise 3: Life Goal Exercise

Based on my present understanding of myself and my present situation, the most important thing related to the purpose in my life is _____

My life goal is _____

_____

Specific goals I can initiate for myself:

1. long-range goal (three years from now) _____

   _____

2. medium-range goal (one year from now) _____

   _____

3. short-range goal (four months from now) _____

   _____

What I will need to accomplish this:

1. external resources (money, help, people, etc.) _____

   _____

2. internal resources (courage, discipline, etc.) _____

   _____

How I typically keep myself from achieving goals: _____

_____

How I can take steps to avoid this: _____

_____

six

Using Your Gifts

Moving is a disorienting experience which uproots us from people and structures which have determined much of our identity. We are forced to grow in new ways, and I firmly believe we are offered a great opportunity to expand our understanding of who God has created us to be and of the potential we have been given. Discovering the meaning of this time of disorientation is crucial and requires us to become engaged in finding and using the gifts God has given us. As we exercise these gifts we shall live God's message of love and reconciliation wherever we are.

The move can be devastating for women who suddenly find themselves at loose ends because they can no longer find outlets for special skills or talents or hold jobs or pursue careers that were a major part of their lives. Sheila (this and following names are fictitious), a nurse, is an example.[18] No matter where she went, she obviously took her healing skills with her, but when she moved to another country, employment restrictions and tax problems made it impossible to work. Many women are unprepared for this kind of sudden narrowing of their options.

Susan was on the threshold of a new time in her life. Her small children were about to enter school, and she had planned to go back to college and train for a new career. The move overseas completely disrupted her plans. The kind of training she sought was unavailable, and, in fact, there were no opportunities at all for schooling in English.

Rebecca had a thriving consulting business. Since she worked free lance, she could pursue her career without the papers required for more structured employment. But it was tough getting established. It took skill, discernment, and persistence to develop a market; yet, she succeeded and was in great demand by the time she returned to the States. In the process she discovered a whole *new* international market for her talents and skills. Thus, this difficult period produced something new in both her personal and professional life.

Judy confided to me that she had always enjoyed being at home, but overseas in a foreign community with an unfamiliar language and different customs, she felt isolated and found it difficult to make friends or become involved in activities which were different from those she had pursued at home. She couldn't seem to find her place or to "plug in" to the new circumstances.

Marie was unable either to pursue her schooling or work as a volunteer in her field. She eventually became embittered and set as her primary goal in The Netherlands a return to the States as soon as possible.

I think also of Peggy, who could no longer use her human relations and conflict management skills professionally, but who discerned a great need within the expatriate community and began to apply her expertise in entirely new ways to a situation which desperately needed her help.

The one experience all these women had in common was an initial loss of self-confidence and identity. They were confused and disoriented because they were in new and different circumstances and lacked the support of familiar structures and friends.

What **do** we have to offer? What is needed? How do we match our gifts to the situation at hand? An exercise, based on Ephesians 4:1-17 and designed to help you begin thinking about these questions, is found at the end of the chapter.

Our unique gifts assist in the task of transmitting the good news that God has created and loves each of us. As we live our lives, we may provoke someone's curiosity about why we are the way we are and lead her to ask more about God.

Our talents are given to us for the good of the community and for the purpose of glorifying God, not just for ourselves. We have all experienced meting out our gifts in exchange for direct benefit to ourselves, whether for money, praise or admiration. At such times we give because we receive a measure of tangible appreciation. But when we use our talents regardless of the benefits to ourselves, we experience pure joy in the giving. I believe that's what God wants for each of us. We have a responsibility to know what gifts we bring to the situation we find ourselves in and then to discern how to use them for the good of the community. When Jesus faced the temptation to use his powers for self-glorification, he countered Satan's efforts by seeking God's honor and glory instead of his own (Matthew 4:1-11).

The risk of using a talent which seems woefully inadequate may look different to us if we realize that where God needs a talent, God provides the means by which that talent or gift will be adequate to meet the need. When food was needed for five thousand, only one small boy with an equally small lunch offered it up to meet the need. The inadequacy was laughable, but Jesus did not laugh. He thanked God for the gift, blessed it, and distributed it, and there was more than enough. God's sufficiency will meet our insufficiency (John 6:5-14).

In Acts 9:36-43 Dorcas was aware of a need shared by many widows of sailors in her town. Although she possessed only one seemingly insignificant talent—sewing—she willingly used it to make them clothing. They were grateful and responded to her with love and affirmation. In fact, they loved her so much that when she died, they called Peter to raise her from the dead. Dorcas' use of her talent to express love and concern for people in need led to glory given to God.

As I have sought to understand what my own talents are, I have learned they are often discovered in situations of need. They may be talents I knew I had already, or they may be talents

I had no idea I possessed but which are called forth through my response to someone else's need. It seems axiomatic that as we are faithful to God's expectation that we will use what we have already, we shall be given more; and as we seek to be responsive to need, we shall receive the necessary talent.

In the parable of the talents in Matthew 25:14-30, the property of the man going on a journey was entrusted to his servants. In the story the property was money, but if we apply this story to our own lives, it could as easily be other possessions, political power, gifts, skills, position, resources—anything which has been entrusted to us. The servants who traded, used, and took risks with that given to them were rewarded with more, but the servant who sought to preserve what was given to him by conserving it was condemned. What did he do wrong? He failed to take risks in using what he had for the good of the master.

There are few other areas of our lives where we are so clearly responsible for our behavior as in using our talents. If we, as the servant in the parable, were asked for an accounting, what could we say? God has entrusted us with an array of abilities, gifts, and resources and has granted us the freedom of choosing to use them. Because overseas moves are often scheduled to last for a designated period of time, many women put their lives on hold, living in a state of suspension instead of applying their skills and using their talents as they would at home. But the length of time you are away has no relationship to how you use the gifts you have. Every day is important, and the growth and feeling of fulfillment you will experience from using your talents and skills in new ways will be well worth the effort.

A friend of mine suggested a marvelous prayer to me: "God, help me to fulfill your vision of my potential." We are all in the process of becoming more tomorrow than we are today. Living in a new place challenges us in that process. Our response is *our* choice.

We are faced with this question: are we willing to respond to a need in which we detect God's call to us whether we think we have the necessary gift or not? We may feel inadequate and therefore seek to avoid the call, or we may have other things we want to do. Let's look at some biblical figures who shared these doubts when called by God.

When God commanded Moses to go to the people in bondage in Egypt and tell them he had been appointed to lead them to the promised land, Moses had a million reasons and excuses why God should choose someone else. He argued with God that he was not a good speaker, that he was slow and hesitant, that he doubted that people would believe God had called him (Exodus 3-4).

When God appointed Jeremiah to be a prophet, he too protested that he could not speak effectively and that he was too young as well (Jeremiah 1).

God persisted in the choice of these men and assured them that the words and the power they needed would be supplied. All that was required of them was their willingness to serve. As we know, both men became giants in proclaiming and exercising God's will among their people.

I have pondered the lives of these and others in the Bible whose position or talent seemed inadequate to meet the task, but who, through their willingness to obey God in spite of overwhelming odds, won great victories. Several questions come to mind.

1. Are we willing to be available to God? In Ezekiel 22:30 God searched for someone to stand in the gap, but no one was found. Because no one was available, the people were doomed. Are we willing to be that one person?
2. Do we limit God by our response? Is our response limited by our preconceptions of the talents we possess and of who we are or should be? Is God's plan delayed because we fail to understand how God could accomplish such a thing through *us*?
3. Do we limit what God can accomplish in our lives because we continue to use proven talents rather than trying something new? Again, how difficult and critical is discernment. There is certainly

validity in saying, "No, that isn't one of my gifts,"
yet it is sometimes equally important to respond,
"Yes, I'll try." Perhaps the key is knowing if this
call fits in with our long-range life goals. If it is
consistent with our goals, perhaps we need to risk
saying yes even without the security of experience
or proven talent. An example in my own life was
when I agreed to form a Bible club for twelve- and
thirteen-year-old boys. It became a surprisingly
wonderful and significant experience for me and
for the boys.

There is a fine line between living harmoniously with
others and being too accommodating and thereby failing to live
up to God's vision of our potential. It takes courage to make an
unpopular decision. We often need to learn the necessity of
"simply going out, not knowing where I am to go" (Hebrews
11:8).

We may never know what we can do until someone asks us,
so we need each other. Gifts are discovered and affirmed in
community. They are found in relationships, recognized by
others, and claimed by ourselves for the purpose of exercising
them for the good of the community.

At the end of the chapter, three biblical exercises will help
you explore the issues discussed here. One examines the choices
Esther made and the consequences of our own life choices. A
second is based on the woman in Proverbs 31 and examines the
use of her talents in her life and provokes thought about the use
of our talents today. Matthew 14:22-33 is the text for the third
exercise, which asks us what new steps Jesus may be calling us
to take.

Women overseas have sought to expand the opportunities
available both to themselves and to others for achieving a
deeper spiritual life. Gien Karssen has offered numerous Bible
study programs focused on women in the Bible who may
provide inspiration and serve as role models. Her books offer
guidelines for starting such groups.[19]

I have been exploring a Bible study method which uses creative activities like writing, drawing, dancing, or sculpting to relate our understanding of the Scriptures to our own lives. The study of Mary and Martha found in chapter 5 is an example of this kind of Bible study.

I would encourage you to form some kind of Bible study group if you feel it will be valuable—and don't worry about whom you will ask to join. When we returned to the States after living in Europe for six years, I had to lead such a Bible study group as a requirement for a course I was taking. I had no idea whom to ask. Most of our friends and neighbors had moved away and we had grown apart from many others. I prayed that God would help me find enough people to form a group. My prayers must have been heard. We had to form two groups!

Another way to connect with others is through a prayer chain in which individual women agree to pray regularly for others in need. A list of such people is maintained by the coordinator of the chain and is passed out periodically. People make their needs known either by calling the coordinator or by leaving a note in the church offering plate.

One "Bloom Where You Are Planted" group combined elements of a prayer group and a support group. (Other Bloom groups, such as the one in Paris, focus solely on orientation programs.) This group was started in Belgium by women who felt the need to pursue disciplined Bible study and intercessory prayer as a focus for developing Christian fellowship. They agreed to read the same scripture and pray daily for each other during the month. A prayer chain was established for special prayer needs, and members were reminded to pray for those who had been transplanted.[20] They posed the following challenges for themselves:

Become part of the greatest force in the world—prayer.
Answer the questions:
> Will others know we are Christians by our love?
> How can we sing the Lord's song in a new land?

Pray each Monday morning at 9:00 A.M. for each other and for specific needs of others outside the group.

Make contact with each other often, if only to say, "I'm thinking of you."

Go out and plant new seeds (i.e., plant friendships with others).

Providing spiritual sustenance is not the only way we can share our gifts or express our talents. Women have established a community mental health help-line, edited a magazine for the American Women's Club, encouraged Americans living overseas to vote, and developed programs to help them become more aware of and knowledgeable about issues of concern to expatriates (new laws affecting children born overseas, for instance).

There is no question that women living overseas have much to contribute and can find a way to do so if they are flexible, perceptive, insightful, and willing to explore new possibilities. But employing our skills and talents will not meet all our needs. Close and meaningful friendships are important too. Many women who have lived abroad for a long time talk of the pain of having to say goodbye over and over again. Knowing that a relationship will be temporary can cause one to hesitate to form deep friendships in order to avoid the pain of certain separation. Yet, the need for intimacy with other people remains. How one makes friendships which can endure these challenges is the subject of the next chapter.

EXERCISES

Exercise 1: The Giving of Gifts (Ephesians 4:1-17)

1. How do you know when you possess a particular gift?
2. Think of times when others have affirmed particular gifts or talents you have. List those which others have identified in you.
3. In which of your particular roles—parent, wife, friend, church member, neighbor, artist, writer, business person, etc.—is it easiest for you to be yourself? In what role is it most difficult?
4. What connections do you see between the roles you are asked to play now and the particular gifts you feel you have?
5. Read Luke 9:62. Are there ways in which you look back to previous times when you played another role or used different gifts? Which gifts that you possess do you need **now** in the roles you play?
6. How can you build up the body of Christ here and now in this place and time as a "purpose of gifts" according to Ephesians 4:12-13?

Exercise 2: The book of Esther

1. What qualities in Esther's character most impress you? How did they make a difference in her life situation?
2. Is there a challenge in your situation similar to that given Esther in chapter 4:13-14? (read also Ezekiel 22:30)
3. What choices did Esther have? What were the possible outcomes of these choices? How could the choice she made have ultimate consequences?
4. What qualities did Esther need in order to choose to follow God in spite of the possible consequences?

5. How can you relate and apply to your own life what you have learned from Esther?

Exercise 3: The Wife of Noble Character (Proverbs, chapter 31)

1. How can we of the twentieth century relate to this woman of ancient times? Think about the areas of home, husband-wife relationship, children, talents.
2. What can you learn from her in the areas of homemaking, use of time, marriage relationship?
3. How could you describe her relationship with her husband—dependent, independent, interdependent? What leads you to this conclusion?
4a. List her talents and skills. How does she develop them both within and outside the home?
4b. What are your talents? List below as many skills as you can recall that you have developed and/or applied in your life—playing the piano, sewing, writing, selling, swimming, being a good listener, etc. Now list those which have given you the most pleasure. Which skills are you using now? Are there some which you are not now using but which you may want to pick up again? How can you develop and/or use them where you are right now? How can you use your gifts to Christ's glory (see Romans 12)?
5. What qualities would you list in describing her character?
6. What is the prime motivation for her life?
7. What is her influence on her family, her children, those beyond her family circle? How do you know this?
8. How can you apply to your own life what you have learned about hers? Be specific.

Exercise 4: Walking on Water (Matthew 14:22-33)

1. What is the most daring thing you have ever done?
2. Why was it daring?
3. When it comes to taking risks, how would you describe yourself—careful, impulsive, daring, scared?
4. What do Peter's actions reveal about his relationship with Jesus?
5. What do you think Jesus meant by *faith* in verse 31?
6. Where in your life do you think God is calling you to "get out of the boat"?
7. What will you do about this?
8. With whom will you share this?
9. How will you hold yourself accountable for taking action?

seven

Being a Friend

DIFFERENT DEFINITIONS OF *FRIEND*

Americans tend to use the term *friend* more loosely than most other national groups. "My friend" may refer to (1) a casual acquaintance living around the corner, (2) someone we meet at the gym where we exercise during the week, (3) a colleague or associate from work, a club, or organization, or (4) someone in whom we have confided our joys and sorrows over several years and with whom we have an ongoing, in-depth relationship. It is this last category for which people in many cultures reserve the word *friend.*

In an interpretation of American and European adult social life, Kandel and Lesser suggest that Americans tend to participate in many friendships at a rather superficial level while Europeans tend to engage in fewer friendships but at a deeper level.[21] Europeans have said to me, "When we call a person a friend, we mean that person is a friend for life."

Understanding this difference in the American's and non-American's meaning of *friend* helps us understand some of the differences in expectations the two groups have when attempting to establish a friendship and the misunderstandings that can occur as the relationship develops. The definition used by Europeans encompasses the quality of the friend relationship I have often felt to be missing in our lives as we moved from place to place. There have been and are people in my life who are friends in that sense. But moving frequently does not provide the conditions conducive to sustaining old, deep friendships or of developing new ones.

A questionnaire distributed by Gien Karssen as part of the research for one of her books on friendship listed the characteristics of a friend. The qualities respondents ranked highest included acceptance, understanding, loyalty, enjoyment, openness, someone who listens, someone to be relied upon, someone who allows freedom for each to be himself/herself.

Many expatriates indicate it is friendship with qualities like those listed above which they miss in an overseas experience. It takes time to share the kinds and numbers of experiences from which trust and commitment grow, and that is time the expatriate doesn't have. People on overseas assignments often protect themselves from the inevitable termination of a meaningful friendship by never beginning one. Many women have told me, "I don't want to begin a good friendship because it hurts too much when one of us has to leave." Another factor which inhibits the development of close friendship is the effort involved. It takes a lot of energy simply to settle into a new lifestyle, particularly when adapting to a new culture, and there is often little energy left to develop in-depth friendships.

Yet there are ways to develop deeper relationships quickly and to sustain them in the face of time limitations. Our family has enjoyed some of our most meaningful friendships overseas and we have often wondered, with our friends, if God took all of us halfway around the world simply to meet each other.

DEVELOPING DEEPER FRIENDSHIPS

Intentionality may be the first requirement. You must **want** to establish a friendship. One Dutch couple with whom

we grew very close worked very hard at developing our friendship, a fact I only realized in retrospect. They dropped in now
and then to see us and chat. They included us in gatherings of
people they thought we would enjoy. They even invited us to
significant family events; for example, because of my interest in
the ministry, they took me to hear their son preach the
candidacy sermon for his pastoral examination. They worked
with us at church on organizing programs and special events of
mutual concern and interest. We enjoyed walking and sightseeing together. They discussed with us happenings in the Dutch
community and asked for our opinions and views. A presentation that I gave one evening stimulated them to rethink their
own ideas, and they invited a group of us to discuss our
thoughts. That lead them to give a presentation that explored
the subject in greater detail. We invited them to join us for
various celebrations and we exchanged cards when we couldn't
get together.

It may seem strange to analyze the building blocks of a
relationship, but there was a day when I realized how close we
felt to these dear friends and how much we treasured our
relationship with them. I wondered how, in a relatively short
time, we could have grown to care for each other so much. I
looked back to see how it had happened and realized that many
small and specific actions comprised the building of our friendship. Sharing common interests was one significant compo-
nent, but perhaps the most important was their **intention** to
reach out to us.

In-depth friendships require a combination of time, availa-
bility, sincerity, sensitivity, concern, and care. A poem written
by one of our local elementary school children captures the
essence of friendship:

A friend is loyal that is true
He is understanding about all you do
To be unselfish is a very good start
But really caring is the very best part

To really care about someone requires empathy. The
American Indians call it "walking in another's moccasins." Our

ability to empathize comes at least in part from an ability to be open to our own feelings, to experience without censure the full range of our own emotions. Without allowing ourselves to experience our own feelings, we will be unable to enter into those of another person. Our understanding will be limited to our idealized versions of who they (or we) should be or what they (or we) should feel. We can feel empathy with another regardless of how long we have known that person or how much or little we have shared. If we are not afraid to feel, we will be able to touch and be real to each other.

TO BE REAL

Listen to the definition of what it means to be real as spoken by the Skin Horse, a stuffed animal in Margery Williams' book, *The Velveteen Rabbit.*

> "Real isn't how you are made," said the Skin Horse. "It's a thing that happens to you. When a child loves you for a long, long time, not just to play with, but REALLY loves you, then you become Real." "Does it hurt?" asked the Rabbit. "Sometimes," said the Skin Horse, for he was always truthful. "When you are Real you don't mind being hurt." "Does it happen all at once, like being wound up," he asked, "or bit by bit?" "It doesn't happen all at once," said the Skin Horse. "You become. It takes a long time. That's why it doesn't often happen to people who break easily, or have sharp edges, or who have to be carefully kept. Generally, by the time you are Real, most of your hair has been loved off, and your eyes drop out and you get loose in the joints and very shabby. But those things don't matter at all, because once you are Real, you can't be ugly, except to people who don't understand."[22]

To be real is to love and to love is to be real. Real friendship is one in which both persons take the risks of being open, daring to let the other share in knowing them as they are inside. It takes a leap of faith to shed our masks. We wonder how we will be perceived by our friend. Will we be rejected? Or worse yet, will we be ignored if we honestly let the other know we're scared or hurting or need help? On the other hand, how will we react to a friend in need? Can we be open enough to really care, and if so, how will he or she react if we show our feelings? That can be threatening too. I believe that shedding our masks is the only way to real life. It does involve bruises and hurts, rejections, and misunderstandings, but it also includes unexpected joys and surprises. We may even discover new depths in our closest relationships.

Listen to Lizzie, a character in the play *The Rainmaker*, talking about her father to a friend.

> Some nights I'm in the kitchen washing the dishes and Pop's playing poker with the boys. Well, I'll watch him real close. And at first I'll just see an ordinary, middle-aged man, not very interesting to look at. And then, minute by minute, I'll see little things I never saw in him before. Good things and bad things—queer little habits I never noticed he had and ways of talking I never paid any mind to. And suddenly I know who he is and I love him so much I could cry. I want to thank God I took the time to see him real.'[23]

That's also how God sees us. Real. God accepts us, even loves us just the way we are. Take the time to see the people in your life, whether they are members of your own family or friends, as real. They are God's gift to you; you are God's gift to them. Let them know you love them. Don't wait until it's too late, until you or they have moved away or until you have somehow just drifted apart. Concentrating on opening up and being real to the other is a way of shortening the time it takes to develop a close friendship and making it more feasible to do so within the time limitations of expatriate living. And even when you separate, you have left something with another which can never be lost and which can be renewed through whatever contact is possible over time.

Long ago when we moved from Southern California, my closest friend wrote me this note: "Though we quit writing and lose verbal contact, you have given me a part of yourself which will always be a part of me. Nothing can change that. That is a most precious gift. Your friend, Chris." The amazing thing is that we do still arrange to see each other. We still write and share the important passages and changes in our lives. Who knows what a difference the gift of yourself may make in another's life?

I have written these words thinking specifically of developing relationships with friends; however, these principles apply to relationship building within the family as well. If we would intentionally take the time to build closer relationships with spouses and children, perhaps we would have less estrangement within families.

THE ART OF LISTENING

One of the basic characteristics of an intimate friendship is the ability of the friends and family members to listen to each other. It has become a rare compliment to be told that you are a good listener. Yet, it is a skill within the capability of us all if consciously cultivated.

To be asked to listen to another is a privilege and a gift. We are given an opportunity, if we choose to take it, to become a facilitator of growth for the person talking **if we listen** to all that is being communicated. So often we think we are listening to each other when in actuality we may hear the words that are being said but fail to listen for the inner meanings and feelings being expressed. Consequently, we miss the message. This usually happens when we are unable to set aside our own preconceptions of the other person or our own feelings about what he or she is saying to fully listen. If we concentrate and focus as completely as possible on the other person, suspending our own agenda and opinions, we will be amazed at the miracle which can take place in each other and in the relationship. It is not easy and it takes much practice, but the reward makes the effort worthwhile.

The process of active listening is described in detail in Dr. Thomas Gordon's book *Parent Effectiveness Training*.[24] Basically it means listening for the *feeling* being expressed instead of listening only to the words being spoken. I can recall times when I have been angered, but in talking to the person with whom I was angry, I diluted the emotion with a smile and soft words. I did not communicate clearly and was not heard. The listener became confused by receiving a mixed message. Miscommunication occurred when the person "listened" as much or more to the smile and soft words than to the feeling I was trying to express. By identifying the feeling through active listening, you are much better able to pinpoint the essence of the message being conveyed. For example, imagine you heard the following message (which is taken directly from a friend's letter after she moved away.): "I don't know what to do with myself without a few familiar faces from home." What might a typical response be? I could imagine responding, "You'll feel better after you have made a few friends." This response essentially denies the feelings being expressed and attempts to soothe the speaker instead. An example of active listening would be to identify the feeling being expressed and then respond to that feeling: "It must be hard to get involved in meaningful activities without your usual friends. It must be lonely." (It is! I miss everyone.) Once the inner feelings have been heard accurately and accepted, the person is free to move on to discover his or her own options within the situation at hand.

Often we unconsciously accept responsibility for another's feelings by attempting to offer advice or comfort instead of letting the sender work out his or her own solution. Even as I write these words, I remember two long-distance phone calls I received within the last twenty-four hours from friends who wanted me to listen to their feelings of pain and frustration about particular situations. Neither one felt she had a friend close by with whom she could share these kinds of feelings and be heard and understood. When one of them asked for my advice, I resisted the temptation to offer my opinion. Instead, I attempted to reflect back her feelings and asked a few clarifying questions. Since I did not know enough about her situation to take the responsibility for suggesting a solution, I trusted her to find her own answer to the problem. As it turned out, she did take a different course of action from what I would have suggested, so I was glad I had not acquiesced to her request to tell her what to do. At the end of the conversation with both friends, each sighed and said, "Thanks for listening." One of them added, "I could only think of two persons with whom I could share this. I'm glad you were there."

Another part of the process of listening is acceptance of both positive and negative feelings. If a person expresses negative feelings, a good listener indicates acceptance of those feelings. It is amazing how many of us are unable to deal with or accept our own negative feelings. When someone else does, there is a greater possibility we can too. I recently wrote to a friend to tell him how very much his acceptance of my angry feelings had been a liberating experience for me. Through his listening to me with care, I was able to accept myself when I felt unacceptable.

If the feelings expressed are positive ones, the listener can reflect them back to the sender, thereby signaling that the person's positive feelings are affirmed and shared. In both instances acceptance and affirmation of the individual and his or her feelings is strengthening to both the person and to the relationship. Marks of an intimate friendship are acceptance of each other and the freedom to be oneself in the relationship; active listening promotes both.

What a loss of potential friendships we experience when we do not learn the art of listening to one another. It is with those one or two people who we know will really listen to us that we feel safe to share our innermost thoughts. Eli Wiesel expresses this idea of friendship well in his book, *The Gates of the Forest*, and although he refers to friend as "brother," I believe we can apply these words to mean "sister" too.

> What is a friend? More than a father, more than a brother: a traveling companion, with him, you can conquer the impossible even if you must lose it later. Friendship marks a life even more deeply than love. Love risks degenerating

into obsession, friendship is never anything but sharing. It is to a friend that you communicate the awakening of a desire, the birth of a vision or a terror, the anguish of seeing the sun disappear or of finding that order and justice are no more. That's what you can talk about with a friend. What is a friend? Someone who for the first time makes you aware of your loneliness and his, and helps you to escape so you in turn can help him. Thanks to him you can hold your tongue without shame and talk freely without risk.[25]

Of course there are times when we cannot listen, when our own needs conflict with taking the time at that moment to hear another. In such cases it is preferable to make a specific commitment to talk later when we know we can be fully present rather than to listen with half an ear. We can all identify times when we have listened impatiently so we could offer our own advice or opinion, or times when we have only half listened, tuning out the speaker while mentally making lists of things to do or fantasizing about this or that. We insert an "uh huh" now and then to assure the other person we are listening, but no one is really fooled; instead we rob ourselves and the speaker of an important opportunity.

To listen to another requires courage. We may be surprised and change our point of view, or we ourselves may be challenged to change. We will need to give up our "right to be right" as well as long-standing habits of listening and responding. It means being willing to set aside our own needs or agreeing on a time when we can be fully present to a friend or family member. Even though we may not be good listeners now, the ability to listen effectively and with care is a skill we can all cultivate. Through the development of this aspect of our friendship, both we and the one to whom we listen will grow. The wonderful moment may come after months of diligently changing our way of listening to a child, for example, when he or she becomes a sensitive listener for the parent who is grappling with a problem. Surprisingly enough, we will find as we learn to listen to another, that we will also grow in the ability to listen to ourselves—and even to God.

THE ABILITY TO CONFRONT

In developing a lasting friendship or family relationship, equally as important as being able to express affirmation for the other is the ability to confront the other in love when differences arise between you.

I used to view confrontation as rejection. I was afraid to confront someone myself, and I saw another's confrontation of me as criticism. It was not until a close friend confronted me about a behavior pattern blocking our ability to relate to each other in a mature and positive way that I realized how much courage it takes to manage confrontations. Contrary to my original interpretation, the act of confrontation is a gift which says, "I love and care about you enough to bring up this difference between us because our relationship is meaningful to me, and I value it." To confront takes courage.

Those of us who live somewhere only a year or two often find it easier to keep a smile on our faces and to avoid confrontations or working through conflicts because we know we will be leaving soon. As one person said to me, "It's not worth it to rock the boat." But is that always true? You will decide some relationships are **not** worth developing, but the relationships you want to be meaningful and lasting require truth and integrity as well as affirmation. Ultimately, we face the question: is it worth the price of missing the potential of this relationship in order to avoid confrontation?

Superficial acceptance, which excludes dealing with the negative, leads to a saccharine or "Pollyanna" relationship. On the other hand, solving conflicts by domination may result in immediate satisfaction for one party but is destructive to the development of a long-lasting, trusting relationship. Either approach creates an atmosphere of dishonesty or distrust, in which relationships wither—be they between friends, colleagues, parents and children, or marriage partners. Indeed, the entire community suffers from unresolved conflicts which fester below the surface, whether in our homes, schools, churches, offices, or other social settings.

In one overseas assignment I experienced differences with another church member. Although I had sought to achieve some kind of mutual understanding, tension continued between us and I decided we probably would not have a long-lasting relationship. I had therefore let it go. But then I heard from a mutual friend in another country that it was common knowledge the two of us did not get along. For the sake of the entire church climate it became imperative that we seek reconciliation, not only for our own benefit but for that of others in the church as well. With much trepidation and fear I confronted the other person. In the exchange—which did clear the air significantly—I heard the other side of the story and realized it contained some truths about myself that I needed to deal with and some changes I needed to make. Out of the confrontation we both grew in mutual understanding and appreciation of each other.

Differences and conflicts of needs, expectations, and desires will be encountered in every close relationship. Many ways of handling such situations—overlooking or repressing conflicts, papering them over, walking away from them, attacking them indirectly through third parties, or simply assuming one is right and the other wrong—incur the high risk of your not being able to develop an open and honest relationship. A better option is to confront the issue in an atmosphere of caring and respect, seeking to understand and retain the integrity of both persons' viewpoints while resolving the differences through a mutually acceptable solution. I have found this to be vital in both friendships and family. It is important, however, to be sensitive to cultural as well as individual differences regarding confrontation. You may find that an indirect approach or even a third party intervention may be more effective with some cultural groups.

Thomas Gordon's *Parent Effectiveness Training* offers some useful guidelines on how to confront issues while at the same time respecting the feelings of both parties. While focused on adult-child relations, the guidelines offer insights into adult-adult relationships as well. Most important is that neither party feels he or she is being forced to change. Each must arrive at the need for change from within.[26] Here is what Gordon suggests.

1. Objectively describe the situation or behavior which is creating the conflict. Try not to blame or pass judgment. "Regulations concerning my department have been issued without my being consulted," or "Dirty pots and pans and open peanut butter and jelly have been left on the kitchen counters."

2. Express yourself in terms of what you **feel** rather than what the other person is doing wrong. "I feel overlooked and ignored," **not** "You always over-look me or leave me out," or "You always put me down." Blaming messages are almost certain to arouse a defensive and/or hostile reaction. By stating how you feel, it is quite possible you are telling the other person something he or she didn't know, and you are much more likely to elicit a positive response.

3. State how you are affected by the situation or behavior. "I am uninformed about the latest policy, and I cannot explain it when those report-ing directly to me question me about it," or "I have to clean up the kitchen after you."

4. Say specifically and unemotionally what you **want.** "I would appreciate it if we could work together to develop new policies." "I would appreciate it if you would wash the pans and counters and put away the peanut butter and jelly after you have eaten."

Again, by refusing to let disagreements, problems or conflicts fester, by habitually confronting them and putting them behind you, you save precious time in the development of friendships in the expatriate situation.

Because the necessity to confront usually involves feelings of anger, it may benefit us to recall Ephesians 4:26: "Be angry but do not sin; do not let the sun go down on your anger, and give no opportunity to the devil." The verse does not say we are not to feel angry; rather, we are to deal with it, to resolve it. What have our previous experiences with anger been, our attitudes about being angry? How have we in the church usually treated anger? In contrast to Jesus, who expressed his feelings of anger and confronted those who aroused that feeling within him (Matthew 21:12-13; Mark 3:4-6), I think we in the church often repress it or cover it in some way. The unfortunate truth is that it then often erupts in other ways—gossip, resentments, "politics." How much healthier it is for all concerned to learn to deal with the conflict before it escalates and causes serious problems for those involved.

In Matthew 5:23-24 we are advised, "So if you are offering your gift at the altar and there remember that your brother has something against you, leave your gift there before the altar and go; first be reconciled to your brother and then come back and offer your gift." What is our responsibility in this situation? Why is the importance of going first to make peace stressed, even if it is the other person who has something against us? What difference will there be in the offering of our gift because we have resolved the conflict in our relationship with another?

Most of us, if we are honest with ourselves, would admit we have conflicts in our relationships that need resolution. Trying the simple conflict resolution exercise found at the end of this chapter is a good starting point for addressing those conflicts.

THE GROWTH OF RELATIONSHIPS

The kind of relationship I have been discussing here is sometimes called "tough love." It involves dealing openly and honestly with everything that happens to the parties in the relationship, respecting each other's individuality, giving and receiving freely, and not only wanting the best for each other but challenging one another to find it.

In reading through the Bible, I am constantly amazed at the example God sets for us of this tough love. God constantly reaches out to us in spite of our rejection or indifference. This open and honest love is a recurring theme throughout the Old Testament, culminating in the life, death, and resurrection of the Son, Jesus Christ, who came to restore our broken relationship with God and with each other. When we seek loving relationships with each other which incorporate and affirm the fullness of our humanity, I believe we become instruments of God's grace.

Quality friendships transcend the limitations of time and space. When we meet again it often seems as though we've never been apart. Strangely enough, being uprooted may be exactly the opportunity we need to **learn how** to form more intimate friendships than we have known previously. Protected by routines and established friendships, the need may never have existed before.

Sometimes I have been surprised by the friendships that I have developed. I have come to realize what a mysterious and wonderful gift friendship is. God does know our needs—"Ask and you shall receive." I believe God will provide all we need, even friends.

EXERCISES

Exercise 1: Friendship Timeline

Think of the relationships in your life which you have
experienced as particularly close. Draw a time line from birth to
the present and divide it into ten-year time segments. In each
time period list those persons whom you would call a friend
from this perspective. It may be that during some times in your
life you had none while at other times you may have enjoyed
several. What did you contribute to the relationship? What did
you receive? If you can identify what you have given and
received in each, you can better understand and be more in
touch with what it is you need from and desire to contribute to
a deep personal relationship. It will also give you clues as to the
kinds of people with whom you are likely to develop a special
friendship.

Exercise 2: Conflict Resolution

Construct for yourself a symbolic altar in a quiet place.
Come before it with a symbolic gift you wish to offer to God.
When you come, stop and think of someone with whom you
have an unsatisfactory relationship. Leave your gift on the altar
and move away from it. Then begin an imaginary dialogue with
the other person in which you attempt to make progress in
resolving your conflict. Use the confrontation and listening
skills I have discussed. When you have finished your initial
statement, change positions and answer as you think the other
person would answer in response to what you have said. Listen
carefully to your words and attempt to empathize with the other
person. Respond to what you heard rather than on the basis of
preconceptions. Continue the conversation until you sense
there is a resolution or at least a movement towards one. Return
to the altar and offer your gift. If you are doing the exercise
alone, record your thoughts and feelings, including any specif-

ics of the conversation you wish. It might work, in fact, to write out your dialogue instead of speaking it. If you're doing it with a small group, talk with the others about your thoughts and feelings. Finally, ask yourself if you feel prompted to talk with (or write to) the other person in your dialogue and follow through on what you've experienced in the exercise.[27]

eight

The Family Circle

Nearly all the women who responded to the questionnaire were concerned about establishing a home, and those with families cited adjustment of the children as a primary issue in moving. The family is a critical focal point during the move, the settling-in process, and the long haul of adaptation. During the adjustment period, especially abroad, the family can be a safe haven, where family members draw support and encouragement from each other. Or it can be a source of misery and tension.

If the stresses involved in the encounter with the new environment and culture are taken out on the family, the chances for a successful adjustment are drastically reduced. This is why families already experiencing marital or parent-child stress should seriously consider the wisdom of making major life moves. Small problems at home usually become larger, and big family problems loom as disasters. People who think that moving somewhere else to start anew is a good strategy should definitely think again. People under stress need an outlet, and those who vent it on family and project the failures or embarrassments or affronts they experience onto family members endanger not only the success of the relocation but the long-term health and stability of the family unit.

If the family is a source of support, it can be a safe haven, a place where members can relax, regroup, find a sympathetic ear for the problems they are encountering, and both give and receive understanding and encouragement. The crux of the matter is the family's attitude about living abroad. If the relocation is truly viewed as an opportunity to learn and grow, to "do a new thing," then family members will be able to draw strength from each other and from their shared faith in God. When the frustrations of culture shock and the loneliness of isolation can be explored and shared, they can be kept in perspective rather than becoming exaggerated and allowed to rule family dynamics.

DEALING WITH CULTURAL ADAPTATION

It is on the wife and mother that the responsibility for a positive family adjustment most often falls; in most cases she is expected to nurture the rest of the family through the adjustment process. If the wife feels secure and confident in the new location, the rest of the family will generally follow suit; but if she is depressed or angry, the family will almost certainly experience difficulties. Unlike her husband , who has an immediate identity from and involvement with his work, and the children, who are engaged in school activities, the wife is often alone (unless there are small children) and left to find her own identity in strange surroundings. In other words, she is expected to nurture her family when she most likely needs nurturing herself. One of the reasons children and husbands rely on the woman for this nurturing is that although the workplace and school provide roles and a structure in which to act them out, those seemingly familiar situations are strewn with subtle cultural pitfalls. The husband must deal with new styles of management (and probably change his own), a multicultural workforce, the host country language, and a clientele that rarely matches the one at home—and he is expected to be productive as he learns how to perform in this new situation.

School is rarely the same as that which was left behind, and although all kinds of support may be provided for the incoming child, there are new procedures to master and new peer groups, often multicultural, to penetrate—in short, entering school in a foreign country is hard work.

The key for the woman's sense of confidence and security is seeing the experience abroad as a challenge rather than a burden, which really is the theme of this book. She plays a very special and critical role in the family's adjustment. But she needs the support of other family members as much as they need hers. Families must more consciously find ways to assist each member and develop a greater level of interdependence than may have been necessary at home. So, how do families become interdependent? After all, many families not only survive the experience abroad but actually flourish. Somehow, being thrust into a new environment seems to make, or perhaps demand, more time to do things together as a family and calls for more creative problem solving. As one woman remarked, "Our family has become more tightly knit because we don't have many outside social contacts and because we are sharing a unique life."

THE INTERDEPENDENT FAMILY

Each family member can make special contributions to the family repertoire of responses to the new environment. Children are especially adept at language learning and can serve as interpreters and help adults with language practice. Through school, they are making acquaintances and friends which may later draw the rest of the family into satisfying relationships. Children need a lot of time and attention during the first weeks abroad and, at least for the first few months, a great deal of help in organizing activities, games, hobbies, and other things to creatively occupy their minds. Many of these can become family projects and often lead to contacts with other expatriate families or with host nationals—the child becomes the focus for discovering ways to become part of the society.

It is only fair to mention that some children never do adjust very well, and it is important for parents to understand it is no one's fault. One family who lived abroad for a year comes to mind. The husband and wife were both teachers, and their children, Susan (nine) and Gary (seven), were enrolled in local schools. Both parents and Susan adapted well and looked on each day as a new adventure. Susan became fluent in the language (often acting as the family translator), made many friends, and delighted in learning local rhymes and games from them. Gary hardly cracked a smile all year and was sullen and withdrawn most of the time, despite the patient and caring support of the family. Once back home, he was his old self again. The experience abroad had not worked for him at his particular age. The family was a haven until he could return to a more comfortable environment.

The husband, through his work, gathers large and valuable quantities of information about the new society which he can transmit to the family. Sometimes it takes some effort to translate what has been learned at work into useful data for the family, but nearly everything that happens there provides an important piece of the cultural puzzle the family is trying to put together. His position may require him to entertain, and this may present unique opportunities to meet and become acquainted with host country nationals as well as a reason for seeking advice on appropriate ways of entertaining business associates.

The wife, meanwhile, is mastering the immediate social and physical environment, helping to make it comprehensible to the others, and facilitating their adaptation to it. While it is difficult to find daily necessities and discover resources within the new society, this quest provides additional pieces to the cultural puzzle and is certainly a source of humorous encounters. The wife and mother comes face-to-face with the culture without institutional cushions and with few guidelines. Her experience may be especially stressful, but it is also rich in cultural data. As noted above, she needs the support that is not available from corporate or school structures and recognition for the unique contributions she makes to the family's culture learning.

Families with teenagers can experience turbulence over value conflicts. Some American parents in Denmark were suddenly confronted with teenagers who wanted the same freedom young Danes have in establishing living arrangements and pursuing sexual relationships. Cultural values and norms were very different. "Why can't I live with my boyfriend?" complained a fifteen-year-old girl to her parents. Finding ways to solve these and other conflicts is not easy. The listening and confrontation skills described in Chapter 7 offer several useful approaches.

Finding a balance between new experiences and traditional values is very important in enabling the family to adapt and yet maintain its cohesion. The challenges of new ideas and values are invigorating, and the family that is receptive to them has a better chance of adjusting well abroad. But that does not mean that the values or traditions that are meaningful to them have to be forfeited, only that they must add new categories of thought to accommodate the new experiences.

The family can thus be a magnet, drawing its members together in mutual support while allowing each member a forum for sharing his or her special perspectives, contacts, and insights and for contributing to the collective strength of the family unit. And there is even greater potential in together calling on God's support which is available for the asking. In the end the strength derived from this kind of unity will help to make anything encountered in the new situation manageable.

SUPPORTIVE FRIENDS

The family can be a haven and an interdependent unit, but it cannot stand totally alone. Developing friendships outside the family is important, not only, as discussed earlier, for each individual's well-being and identity, but as a support to the family unit. Friends and relatives have been left at home, and they are missed. No longer can grandparents, aunts, uncles, and cousins gather for special events or be with you in times of need. Creating surrogate families with whom you can share may fill the void. One New Year's vacation we joined two other families in Paris for a retreat. We planned a vacation but we also designed activities that included discussing subjects we had decided were important to us, showing family slides, and sharing family histories. We did several biblical exercises, including the one on gifts (Ephesians 4:1-17), and we all drew pictures of the special gifts each of us felt we possessed (e.g., honesty, humor, ability to listen, patience) and brainstormed ways we could share them within our individual families. This was not exactly the kind of spontaneous sharing we had all come to expect from our families at home, but it was a way to allow the sharing and a step toward spontaneity.

On the other hand, you may enjoy the freedom from family involvments and the opportunity to create new ways of relating to others. One woman suggested this when she said, "My family is intense. I've been glad to be away, and now I have to face a lot I haven't had to deal with for the past several years as we move back home." Being away may be an opportunity to develop new patterns of interaction within your family and a time to consciously decide how you want to relate to the extended family when you return home. Instead of a surrrogate family, you may want to discover an entirely new system for including others in your life that meets your needs and provides an alternative to old patterns.

Whatever the motivation or approach to seeking friends of the family, the manner in which these relationships develop will necessarily differ from the way similar relationships unfolded at home. There will be chances to explore new traditions and unfamiliar ways of interacting with people from the host culture and opportunities to develop friendships with compatriots in a new setting and in unusual circumstances. This calls for greater intentionality and more patience than have ever been needed before.

CHALLENGES AND OPPORTUNITIES

Like many couples, Jerry and I consciously wanted to fill our "life scrapbooks" with memories that would bond our family in a special way. We selectively chose from the many opportunities available to us abroad to create those memories. Neither of us had experienced many vacations in our childhood, so we decided to take vacations that our children would always remember. There was a multiplicity of choices. We decided to focus on ancient civilizations: Egypt, Greece and Israel. That decision arose primarily from my boredom with the study of ancient history and art in school. I hoped our sons would find those studies more interesting if we had traveled in these countries. However, we never expected them to be so interested. In Pompeii we dragged ourselves after two boys intent on seeing every overturned rock and ruin while the temperature climbed to 130 degrees. We followed them only because we feared losing them permanently! But it seems our motive for our travel program succeeded. Matthew declared a double major in college: architecture and, yes, history; his course load included as many as four ancient history courses in one year. It takes some planning to gain maximum benefits from travel. At the close of this chapter are suggestions for organizing the collection of memories during vacation trips and on outings within the host country.

Taking trips together provided opportunities for projects then and for special conversations and memories now. Different families will have different interests and other imperatives around which to devise projects that fit them, but the important point is creating special experiences that will live on in family memory. Our slides, photographs, scrapbooks, and memorabilia spark discussions that continually cement our family ties in unique ways.

As a parent you may have visions of your children growing up as international citizens. But you may see them wanting only to be involved with school activities and other expatriate children. They may show no interest in the local culture or young people. Surprisingly, just exposing them to what they can tolerate will help them learn from their experiences and, just as important, from your attitude toward and experience with the host culture. They will almost certainly have a broader worldview although it may not become evident for some years. The influence of the overseas experience on you may become more quickly evident, but it is often still just the beginning of a process. Most families I have known who have participated in some significant way in the new culture have changed, and the change has generally been more profound at subtle levels than at the obvious level of new customs or traditions. Their faith has deepened; they have discovered new directions, adopted new perspectives, and devised new ways of relating. They have evolved toward fuller or expanded self-definitions of themselves as individuals and as a family.

The challenges and opportunities for families living abroad are many; our family certainly experienced difficulties and frustrations while moving, and there were times of loneliness and conflict, but we gained much more than we lost. In the end the words from Isaiah come back to us, "Behold, I am doing a new thing."

EXERCISES

Exercise 1: Developing Family Friendships

Sharing holidays is a nice way to begin developing relationships with people in the expatriate and host communities. We were often invited to share in special holidays with our friends from the host culture, which provided wonderful opportunities to understand our new friends and their culture and country. Similarly, we enjoyed sharing our holidays, deciding as a family to share a particular holiday and selecting people to invite so that everyone felt they had been involved in planning the event. You may want to invite both host nationals and expatriate friends so they can meet each other and to include people from all age groups as well as single people who may especially appreciate sharing a holiday.

Choose a holiday that has special meaning for your family (Thanksgiving, Fourth of July, Christmas) and is celebrated in ways particular to your culture. Sharing family traditions is especially important. For example, we always give each person at the Thanksgiving table three kernels of popcorn. We then ask each to share three things for which they are thankful and then place the corn in one bowl to be popped (with additional popcorn!) and eaten together later. New acquaintances from the host culture will be curious about special foods that are served, the meaning of the holiday in your country, and the family traditions associated with it. Pictures or stories of past holidays can be shared as well.

Holidays not celebrated in the host country provide interesting learning experiences for local acquaintances and friends. Holidays such as Christmas, which may be shared by both cultures, provide opportunities for comparing observances in both cultures.

Exercise 2: Memorable Trips

Sightseeing and vacation trips can be more than a temporary escape from the daily routine, breaks everyone needs in fairly regular doses. They become part of the memories and family lore that we all carry through life. We have found that approaching our trips in a systematic way, especially when living abroad where there are so many opportunites for once-in-a-lifetime travel, has helped us choose destinations more creatively and become more aware of our experiences and more deliberate in collecting memories and memorabilia. The strategy we have used in planning memorable trips involves the basic steps listed below. You can adapt them to your situation.

1. List all the places you would each like to visit on a large sheet of paper. Everyone's ideas can be listed no matter how far or how near the destination, how long or short the time, or how expensive the trip.
2. Divide the suggested destinations into the following categories: day trips, weekend trips, and vacation trips. The last category can be subdivided according to financial and time commitments necessary.
3. Prioritize the suggested trips within each category. Some may be eliminated because limited financial resources or other conditions make them impractical for the foreseeable future.
4. Select destination(s) for the immediate future, then put the list away until your next opportunity to travel.
5. Involve as many family members as possible in making the arrangements and preparing for the trip, including finding information about the destination and sharing it with other members of the family.

We also developed a method for collecting memorabilia, recording our experience, and then organizing everything in a scrapbook after the trip. We all found we learned more and had more fun by following these steps:

1. Provide a large manila envelope for each family member for postcards, travel folders, bills from restaurants, money, stickers, match books, etc.
2. Keep journals during the trip either on separate sheets of paper or in a notebook from which pages can be easily extracted. Ultimately, these pages are pasted into a scrapbook at the appropriate place along with collected items and photos.
3. Take pictures. One of our sons took prints, the other took slides, and Jerry made movies—our trips were well documented.
4. Allow each person to select one artifact or item that is most representative of the area and will provide each one with a cherished remembrance of the place. Jerry and I often combined our purchases into one item for our home—a painting, for example.
5. Upon return, put together a scrapbook for that trip. We learned a lot from our Dutch friends, who are masterful scrapbook makers. In the end we had a family "masterpiece," including journal entries, photos, and items from the manila envelopes along with captions or cartoons and drawings.

Exercise 3: Meaningful Journeys

Jesus and his disciples took many trips, frequently walking from town to town and always talking with and observing the people in regions they visited. Descriptions of those encounters are found in scripture and some are used in exercises in this book; for example, the Canaanite woman, the woman of Samaria. Jesus was especially astute at drawing on the everyday experiences of the people he encountered to illustrate how people can be more caring in their relationships with each other and how they can carry out God's plan.

Early in his ministry, Jesus went to the town of Galilee, where he spoke to the disciples of John the Baptist. He asked them what they went to the desert to see and reminded them that they were searching for a prophet. Although he was referring specifically to John the Baptist, he was also concerned about looking beyond what is easily seen to discover the deeper meaning. Travelers can become so intent on observing those who "wear fine clothes" or searching for "kings' palaces" that they fail to learn from the foreign culture or to grow personally from their experience. Jesus suggests that we look beneath the surface for the truth and for what it means in our lives. Tom Duggan has observed about people living overseas, "In reflecting on life abroad, these people are doing more than acquiring happy memories for their mental scrapbooks. They are reflecting on the meaning of their own lives."[28] Every experience, whether in day-to-day living or traveling to other countries, contributes to this reflection.

Read Matthew 11:1-10 and think about the following questions. You may want to discuss them together as a family, in a small group, or perhaps with one other person.

1. What was the most meaningful trip you have ever taken and why was it meaningful?
2. What did you go there to see? Were your expectations met? What did you see that was surprising?
3. What unexpected meaning did you find through observing the behavior of people you met?
4. In what ways did you learn the most about the foreign culture? About your own culture?

nine

New Beginnings

Recently we learned that an English family had moved to New Jersey from the same town where we had lived in The Netherlands. We invited them to supper as we wanted to make them feel at home and to provide information about the neighborhood and school, to answer any other questions they might have, and to suggest shopping places, doctors, dentists, and so on. Despite the fact that they spoke the language, the United States was a new country for them and there were bound to be many differences to which they would have to adjust.

We answered a myriad of questions, much to everyone's enjoyment, but what struck us most was that this family was involved in another new beginning. They had moved after eighteen months in The Netherlands and expected to be in the United States only two years. Their visit reemphasized for us the awareness of this characteristic experience of overseas living: you just get settled and established when off you go again, either to move to a new location or return home.

Beginnings are often happy and exciting—birth, marriage, a new job or promotion, a new school, a move to a new location. Other beginnings come in the guise of endings—

death, divorce, a move away from beloved family and friends. They may be bitter and lonely endings, but within them are also new beginnings. Not always easy or happy, beginnings may require the development of a new lifestyle, a new attitude, and new kinds of self-discipline. They may be caused by external circumstances or come as a result of your own decisions. You can decide to make a new beginning today. It can be as simple as accepting the present and refusing to look back to the "good old days" or to say, "If only...." It means accepting the possibilities and potential inherent in the present, determining your goals and direction and then saying yes to all that affirms them and no to that which denies their fulfillment. Sam Keen expressed it poignantly in his book *To A Dancing God*:

> I am so many, yet I may be only one. I mourn for all the selves I kill when I decide to be a single person. Decision is cutting off, a castration. I travel one path only by neglecting many. Actual existence is tragic, but fantastic existence (which evades choice and limitation) is pathetic. The human choice may be between tragedy and pathos, Oedipus and Willy Loman. So I turn my back on small villages I will never see, strange flesh I will not touch, ills I will not cure, and I choose to be in the world as a husband, a father, an explorer of ideas and styles of life. Perhaps Zorba will not leave me altogether. I would not like to live without dancing, without unknown roads to explore, without the confidence that my actions were helpful to some.[29]

Every yes includes a no and every no affirms a yes. What does a yes mean for you today? Does it mean living in the present moment fully, finding out why you are here and what you can give and receive in the community? We would do well to listen to the prophet Jeremiah. In Jeremiah 29 he writes to the captives of Israel living in Babylon. They had been carried off from their homeland and, like many of us, were living in a foreign country. They were discouraged and depressed, as voiced in their lament (Psalms 137:1-4):

By the rivers of Babylon we sat down and wept
    when we remembered Zion.
On the willow trees there
    we hung up our lyres
For there our captors
    required of us songs
And our tormentors, mirth, saying
    "Sing us one of the songs of Zion."
How shall we sing the Lord's song in a foreign land?

The advice Jeremiah gave them was not advice for just passing through or marking time. His words reflect commitment and investment of self and time and talents.

> Thus says the Lord of hosts, the God of Israel, to all the exiles whom I have sent into exile from Jerusalem to Babylon: Build houses and live in them; plant gardens and eat their produce. Take wives and have sons and daughters; take wives for your sons, and give your daughters in marriage, that they may bear sons and daughters; multiply there, and do not decrease. But seek the welfare of the city where I have sent you into exile and pray to the Lord on its behalf, for in its welfare you will find your welfare....For I know the plans I have for you, says the Lord, plans for welfare and not for evil, to give you a future and a hope. Then you will call upon me and come and pray to me, and I will hear you. You will seek me and find me; when you seek me with all your heart, I will be found by you, says the Lord.... (Jeremiah 29:4-7, 11-14).

This passage advises putting down roots, even in a place of exile, and making meaningful commitments to the community, seeking its welfare and praying for it. Insert the name of the town where you are living as you say that sentence: "Seek the welfare of———and pray for it." Jeremiah's advice to the Israelites in the sixth century B.C. is just as significant for us today.

When you invest yourself in a new place, a new venture, or a new friendship, the more you give, the more you stand to lose if and when it ends. But through the giving you come to know more about yourself and others and to grow in your knowledge of God. For me the investment and the risk are worth it. Today can be a new beginning. You are the only one who can make that decision for yourself.

Through the prophet Isaiah, God has spoken the following words to us: "Remember not the former things nor consider the things of old. Behold I am doing a new thing. Now it springs forth; do you not perceive it?" (Isaiah 43:18-19) I heard these words after our first major move from my California birthplace to what then seemed the farthest reaches of the universe—New Jersey. It was a promise to me that God was in this new place, that God was at work, and that I needed only to open my eyes to see the new things. If I had sought to duplicate what I had experienced at home in California, I would have missed the new opportunities God had for me in the present. That lesson has been a helpful reminder to me as we have continued to move more often and further away from home.

Perhaps your new beginning will be to find out who God is and what God means in your life. The greatest new beginning of my life came from daring to say yes to God. It was scary. New beginnings usually are. They are unknown, fearful, exciting, promising, and wonderful. Most of all they are up to each of us individually. We are the only ones who can decide to take the first step in a new direction. We may fall or slip backwards. We may even change direction, but the decision to begin will lead to new and unforeseen experiences which we will never know otherwise.

Think about your life since you said, "Yes, I'll move overseas." Using exercise 1, "Reflections on a Walk to Emmaus," which appears at the end of this chapter, reflect on the changes which have taken place in your life since that decision. Talk over your discoveries with others. Take some time to think about the direction your life has taken and your own new beginnings. Return later to this book and especially to exercise 1 and evaluate what has happened; then reexamine your goals and directions with exercise 2.

When God took the Israelites out of slavery in Egypt, they wandered in the wilderness for forty years. Forty years! Not exactly swift or to the point, but God's plans and timing are not ours, and that is where faith and trust come into the picture. Abraham went out not knowing where he was to go. So must we. Recently I heard this prayer which is appropriate for new beginnings. Unfortunately, I do not know its source:

> Lord, today our calendar for the months ahead is as fresh and as clean as we ourselves could be if only we tried more often to live as you would have us live. We know that this is possible, for you are our forgiving parent, God of the second chance, the one who promises that we can always make a fresh beginning. Today as a new day dawns, Lord, let us begin.

EXERCISES

Exercise 1: Reflections on a Walk to Emmaus

   1. Read Luke 24:13-35.

> On that same day two of them were going to a village
> named Emmaus, about seven miles from Jerusalem,
> and they were talking to each other about all the
> things that had happened. As they talked and dis-
> cussed, Jesus himself drew near and walked along
> with them; they saw him, but somehow did not
> recognize him.

When have you walked with Jesus so concerned with your own
pain that you didn't even know He was there?

   2. Since moving overseas what changes have you had
       to make in
           your lifestyle?
           your family?
           the way you spend your time?
           other ways?
   3. What have the advantages been for you and your
       family?
   4. What have the disadvantages been for you and
       your family?
   5. What doors were closed?
   6. What new opportunities became available?
   7. What has been good or growth-producing in your
       life as a result of the above changes you have had
       to make? What evidence is there of resurrection or
       of new life? What denies resurrection or new life?
   8. What suggestions would be most helpful to give a
       friend planning an overseas move?
   9. Like the disciples in the passage above, how were
       your eyes opened to Jesus' presence with you?
       What was the "breaking of the bread" for you?

Exercise 2: An Opportunity for Periodic Reflection and Evaluation

1. Looking back on your overseas experience thus far, what has been most meaningful for you and why?
2. What has your most important realization been?
3. What changes have you made in your life as a result of this transition?
4. How have you taken steps to realize any goals you had set for this time?
5. How have you hindered yourself?
6. How can you remove some of the blocks?
7. What has been the greatest benefit to you as a result of this move?
8. What has been the greatest benefit to your family?

appendix

QUESTIONNAIRE ON ADJUSTMENT OF WIVES LIVING OVERSEAS

Please answer all questions. Your feelings are important to the value of this research. You are completely anonymous unless you choose to identify yourself. If you would be willing to be interviewed, either individually or as a part of a group discussion, please give your name and address. Your experiences would be of great use in the completed project. Please use the back of the questionnaire for further comments. RETURN THE COMPLETED QUESTIONNAIRE WITHIN ONE WEEK'S TIME. Thank you for your participation.

Personal Data

1. Nationality _____
2. Number of years married _____
3. Number of children _____
4. Ages of children_____   _____   _____   _____   _____
5. Do you have children in your home country of origin? _____
6. Do your children attend a local school of the country in which you presently live? _____

130

7. If not a local school, what type? _____

    _____

8. Your age: 25-35_____

    9. 35-45_____   10. 45-55_____   11. Over 55_____

12. Years of education you have completed: High School_____

    13. University years completed 1 2 3 4 14. Graduate school years completed_____

15. In country of origin, did you attend school?_____ If yes, was it full time?_____ 16. Part time?_____

17. If yes to 15 or 16, were you a candidate for a degree? Yes_____ 18. No_____

19. In country of origin, did you work? _____ If yes, was it full time?_____ 20. Part time?_____

Mark the average degree of involvement in these activities at present in hours per month.

Community Activities:

21.   more than 20___   22. 10-20___   23. 5-10___   24. 0-5___

Religious Activities:

25.   more than 20___   26. 10-20___   27. 5-10___   28. 0-5___

Clubs/Organizations:

29.   more than 20___   30. 10-20___   31. 5-10___   32. 0-5___

Children's School:

33.   more than 20___   34. 10-20___   35. 5-10___   36. 0-5___

Adult Education:

37.   more than 20___   38. 10-20___   39. 5-10___   40. 0-5___

Life Overseas

41.   Country you are now living in:_____

42.   How long have you been here?_____

43.   How long do you expect to be here?_____

44.   Purpose for being here (e.g., married to native of this country, one-year business assignment for husband, armed forces, etc.) _____

      _____

45.   Describe previous overseas life (e.g., never, once before for two years in Denmark, etc.) _____

      _____

Circle the number which most closely represents your degree of adjustment in the following areas on a scale of 1-10. 1 represents "easy"; 5 represents "moderately difficult"; and 10 represents "very difficult."

Language:

46.   1   2   3   4   5   6   7   8   9   10

Lifestyle/Culture:

47.   1   2   3   4   5   6   7   8   9   10

Leaving family behind:

48.   1   2   3   4   5   6   7   8   9   10

Feeling cut off from family in home country, especially when problems arise:

49.   1   2   3   4   5   6   7   8   9   10

Leaving friends behind:

50.   1   2   3   4   5   6   7   8   9   10

Leaving children behind:

51.   1   2   3   4   5   6   7   8   9   10

Feeling alone or left behind when first friends you made in this country leave:

52.   1   2   3   4   5   6   7   8   9   10

Finding areas in which to pursue your interests:

53.   1   2   3   4   5   6   7   8   9   10

Interrupting a job or career or school program:

54.   1   2   3   4   5   6   7   8   9   10

Your husband's travel schedule at present:

55.   1   2   3   4   5   6   7   8   9   10

Keeping house (e.g., different appliances, no appliances, shopping, etc.):

56.   1   2   3   4   5   6   7   8   9   10

Integration into the community of residence:

57.   1   2   3   4   5   6   7   8   9   10

Integration into community of home country abroad:

58.   1   2   3   4   5   6   7   8   9   10

What has helped you the most to adjust? Rank in order of 1 (most important) to 4 (least important).

59.   Women's clubs___ 60. Individuals___ 61. Church___ 62. School___
Which of the following programs would help you adjust?

63.   Orientation program___ Describe what would be the most helpful type _____

64. Discussion groups aimed toward personal growth, value clarification, goal setting, communication skills _____

65. Job file (volunteer and paid) _____

66. Small groups for prayer, sharing, fellowship _____

67. Would you use individual counseling resources if available by persons trained, experienced and knowledgeable in overseas living? Yes___ 68. No___

69. Would you participate in small group workshops for personal growth and sharing of ways to cope and adjust if available and led by persons trained, experienced and knowledgeable in overseas living? Yes___ 70. No___

Mark average degree of involvement in these activities at present in **hours per month.**

Community Activities (community of country of residence):

71. more than 20___ 72. 10-20___ 73. 5-10___ 74. 0-5___

Community Activities (in your home country's community here)

75. more than 20___ 76. 10-20___ 77. 5-10___ 78. 0-5___

Religious Activities:

79. more than 20___ 80. 10-20___ 81. 5-10___ 82. 0-5___

Clubs/Organizations:

83. more than 20___ 84. 10-20___ 85. 5-10___ 86. 0-5___

Children's School:

87. more than 20___ 88. 10-20___ 89. 5-10___ 90. 0-5___

Adult Education:

91. more than 20___ 92. 10-20___ 93. 5-10___ 94. 0-5___

Rank those activities in which you are involved in order of satisfaction level—1 represents most satisfying and 6 represents least satisfying. If you do not participate in an activity, mark NA, representing "not applicable."

95. Community Activities (country of residence)___

96. Community Activities (home country's community here)___

97. Religious Activities___

98. Clubs/Organizations___

99. Children's School___

100. Adult Education___

101. Being forced into new situations often produces growth in new and/
      or unexpected areas. What is the area where you personally have
      grown the most as a result of this move? _____

102. What is the most important issue for you at this moment in your life?
      _____
      _____
      _____

103. What are the benefits you have most experienced as a result of living
      here? _____
      _____
      _____

104. What were your worst fears prior to coming? _____
      _____
      _____
      _____

105. Have those fears been true or unfounded? How do they correlate with
      the actual situation? _____
      _____
      _____

Use the space below and/or the back of the questionnaire for ideas you wish
to share. If you wish to be interviewed, please write your name and address.
THANK YOU for sharing your life experience!

Endnotes

1. Meyer, *Great Men*, 71.

2. Paddy Welles, private letter to the author.

3. Raines, *To Kiss the Joy*, 9-10.

4. Gail Duggan. Comments from a talk delivered at the 1984 Pastors and Spouses Conference, Association of International Churches in Europe and the Middle East, Brussels, May 1984.

5. Johnson, *Congregations As Nurturing Communities*, 3.

6. Carolyn Connors, private letter to author.

7. Janssen, *A Comparative Study*, 4.

8. Goodstein, "Human Relations Training," 161.

9. Susan Dyer, human relations specialist in The Hague, The Netherlands, has shared this model with me.

10. Holmes and Raye, *The Social Readjustment Scale*, 213-18. Mine is an adaptation of the Holmes and Raye scale.

11. Kohls, *Survival Kit for Overseas Living*, 72-73.

13. Baker, *Wooden Shoes*, 138-39.

14. This exercise is adapted from Lanto, *The Life Planning Workbook*, ch. 2.

15. Welles, *Trials and Tribulations of Transplantation*, 7.

16. Interpretations of Maslow's Triangle appear in Gordon, *The Basic Modules of the Instructor Outline for Effectiveness Training Courses,*

F-8. Dr. Gordon and Effectiveness Training Associates have also written and designed books and training courses for teachers (T.E.T.), clergy (C.E.T), business and other leaders (L.E.T.), and women (E.T.W.) Information about these materials can be obtained from Effectiveness Training Associates, Instructor Training Deptartment, Solana Beach, CA 92075. (714) 481-8121. In particular you might want to inquire about Effectiveness Training for Women by Linda Adams (see bibliography).

16. Lanto, *op. cit.*, adapted from chapters 6 and 7.

17. This exercise has been developed as a result of training with Walter Wink. See his book, *Transforming Bible Study*, listed in the bibliography for more explanation of how to use this approach.

18. Individuals are not named to preserve anonymity.

19. See particularly Karssen, *Her Name Is Woman*, 13-17.

20. Experiences described in the "Bloom Where You are Planted" program of The American Church of Antwerp, Belgium; private letter to author.

21. Kandel and Lesser, *Youth in Two Worlds*, 172.

22. Williams, *The Velveteen Rabbit*, 16-17.

23. Nash, *The Rainmaker*, Act 3, Line 179, 131.

24. Gordon, *Parent Effectiveness Training*, 49-55. Another excellent resource on the skills of listening is Reuel L. Howe's *The Miracle of Dialogue* (see bibliography).

25. Wiesel, *The Gates of the Forest*, pp. 36-37.

26. Gordon, *Parent Effectiveness Training*, pp. 103-147.

27. Wink, *Transforming Bible Study*, 64-65.

28. Duggan, *A Strategy for Ministry for Newcomers*, 14.

29. Keen, *To a Dancing God*, 119-20.

Biblical References

Biblical quotes are taken from the Revised Standard Version unless otherwise noted. All quotes are reworded to embrace inclusive language.

Chapter 1

Acts 17:26-27 And God made from one every nation of people
Luke 9:62 No one who puts the hand to the plow and looks back
Isaiah 43:18-19 Remember not the former things nor consider

Chapter 2

Mark 9:14-29 I believe. Help thou my unbelief
Psalms 139 Lord, you have examined me and you know me
Matthew 25:31-46 When the Son of man comes in his glory

Chapter 3

Isaiah 43:18-19 Do not cling to the events of the past (*Today's English Version*)
Genesis 12-22 Now the Lord said to Abram
Genesis 12:1 Go from your country
Genesis 12:2 And I will make you a great nation
Genesis 15:3 Behold, thou hast given me no offspring
Genesis 16:1-3 Sarah, Abraham's wife, bore him no children
Genesis 22:1-18 After these things God tested
James 2:23 Abraham believed God
Ruth 1:16-17 Where you go, I will go
Genesis 37-50 Jacob dwelt in the land of his father's sojournings
John 15:16 You did not choose me
John 4:7-42 There came a woman of Samaria
Matthew 15:21-28 And Jesus went away from there
1 Kings 17:8-24 Then the word of the Lord came
Acts 11:5-17 I was in the city of Joppa praying

Chapter 4

1 Kings 19:1-18 Ahad told Jezebel all that Elijah had done
Romans 13:8-10 Owe no one anything
Mark 5:1-20 They came to the other side of the sea

Chapter 5

Esther 4:13-14 Think not that in the king's palace
Nehemiah 1-2 O Lord God of heaven
Psalms 25:12 Who is the person who fears the Lord
Colossians 1:9-12 For this reason, we have always prayed for you
Luke 10:38-42 Now as they went on their way
John 11:1-45 Now a certain man was ill
John 12:1-8 Six days before the passover

Chapter 6

Ephesians 4:1-17 I therefore, a prisoner for the Lord
Matthew 4:1-11 Then Jesus was led up by the spirit
John 6:5-14 Lifting up his eyes
Acts 9:36-43 Now there was at Joppa a disciple
Matthew 25:14-30 For it will be as when
Exodus 3-4 Now Moses was keeping the flock
Jeremiah 1 The words of Jeremiah
Ezekiel 22:30 And I sought for one among them
Hebrews 11:8 By faith Abraham obeyed
Proverbs 31 The words of Lemuel, King of Massa
Romans 12 I appeal to you therefore
Matthew 14:22-23 Then he made the disciples get into the boat
Luke 9:62 No one who puts the hand to the plow

Chapter 7

Ephesians 9:26 Be angry but do not sin
Matthew 21:12-13 And Jesus entered the temple of God
Mark 3:4-6 Is it lawful on the sabbath to do good
Matthew 5:23-24 So if you are offering your gift

Chapter 8

Ephesians 4:1-17 I therefore, a prisoner for the Lord
Matthew 11:7-10 As John's disciples were leaving, Jesus (*The Student's Bible*)
Matthew 11:1-19 After Jesus had finished instructing (*The Student's Bible*)

Chapter 9

Jeremiah 29 These are the words of the letter
Psalms 137:1-4 By the rivers of Babylon we sat down and wept

Jeremiah 29:4-7,11-14 Thus says the Lord of Hosts
Isaiah 43:18-19 Remember not the former things
Luke 24:13-35 That very day two of them

Bibliography

Ackerman, James S. "Why Sojourn in a Foreign Land?" Sermon preached in Tenafly, NJ, 20 June 1980.

Adams, Linda. *Effectiveness Training for Women, E.T.W.* New York: Putnam, 1979.

Adler, Peter T. "The Transitional Experience: An Alternative View of Culture Shock." *Journal of Humanistic Psychology* 15 (Fall 1975): 22.

Backalenick, Irene. "In the Corporate World, Men Move Up, but Families Just Move." *New York Times,* 29 December 1973.

Baker, Victoria J. *Wooden Shoes and Baseball Bats.* Leiden, The Netherlands: ICA Publications 63, 1982.

Bowers, Barbara. "Brussels Community Service Helps Foreigners Cope." *International Herald Tribune,* 28 August 1979.

Brown, Robert McAfee. *Creative Dislocation–The Movement of Grace.* Nashville: Abingdon, 1980.

Buchanan, Sherry. "Firms Count Cost of Failing to Study Expatriate Stress." *International Herald Tribune,* 26 June 1985.

——."How Some Firms Handle Stress of Transfer Abroad." *International Herald Tribune,* 3 June 1985.

Campbell, Edward F., Jr. *Ruth, A New Translation with Introduction and Commentary.* New York: Doubleday & Co., 1985.

Carpenter, Harold. "Reentry: The Unexpected." *Mountain Movers* (April 1983): 9-10.

"Check List for Families on the Move." *Lutheran Witness* (July 1980).

Christensen, Inge F. "Reverse Culture Shock." Report from Federation of Women in Countries Overseas, London, March 1979.

Cody, R. Dixie. "Questionnaire Survey of Wives Living in Stavanger, Norway." Manuscript. Stavanger, Norway.

"Coming Home Again: Absorbing Culture Shock." *Infogram.* Provo, UT: Brigham Young University Language Center, 1981.

"Coping Overseas." *International Herald Tribune,* 7 December 1979.

"Cross-Cultural Quiz." *Bridge* (Summer 1978): 19-20.

Darrow, Ken, Dan Morrow, and Brad Palmquist. *Transcultural Study Guide.* Stanford, CA: Volunteers in Asia, 1975.

Discipleship Journal. Colorado Springs, CO, bimonthly.

Duggan, Thomas E. *A Strategy for Ministry for Newcomers.* D. Min. thesis, Princeton University, 1977.

Ferguson, Faith. "Cultural Re-Entry, the Surprise Package." *American Women's Club Magazine,* The Netherlands (May 1983): 11-13.

Fields, W.J. "Problems Facing Families Transferred Overseas." *Geneva Church Monthly Magazine,* Geneva, Switzerland (Summer 1979).

Friedman, James. "Americans Overseas: A Few are Happy." *International Herald Tribune,* 23 May 1979.

Gamarekian, Barbara. "U.S. Diplomats' Wives Feel They Should Be Paid." *International Herald Tribune,* 18 April 1984.

"Gauging a Family's Suitability for a Stint Overseas." *Business Week* (16 April 1979).

Gaylord, Maxine. "Relocation and the Corporate Family." *Bridge* (Winter 1979): 3.

Gibbs, Terri A. "Finding a Sense of Belonging in Your New Place." *Evangelical Missions Quarterly* (July 1980): 159-65.

Goodstein, L.D. "Human Relations Training." In *Encyclopedia of Psychology,* Vol. 2, edited by Raymond J. Corsini. New York: John Wiley & Sons, 1984.

Gordon, Thomas. *P.E.T., Parent Effectiveness Training.* New York: Peter H. Wyden, Inc., 1970.

——.*The Basic Modules of the Instructor Outline in Effectiveness Training Courses.* Pasadena, CA: Effectiveness Training Associates, 1971.

Herz, Martin, F., ed. *Diplomacy: The Role of the Wife, A Symposium.* Washington, DC: Institute for the Study of Diplomacy, Georgetown University, 1981.

Hill, Martha. "A Parent's Guide to Moving." U.S. Foreign Service, n.d.

Holmes, Thomas, and Richard Raye. "The Social Readjustment Scale." *Journal of Psychosomatic Research.* 2, no. 2 (August 1967).

Howe, Reuel L. *The Miracle of Dialogue.* New York: Seabury Press, 1963.

Janssen, Gretchen. "A Bible Club." *The Small Group Letter*, 1, no. 7 (November/December 1984).

——. *A Comparative Study of Cross-Cultural Experiences of Contemporary Women.* Master's thesis, Union Theological Seminary, New York City, 1986.

——. "Challenges and Opportunities of Living Overseas." *American Women's Club Magazine*, The Netherlands (Sept. 1981-June 1982).

——. "Reactions and Adjustments of Teenagers Moving to Denmark." Manuscript.

——. "Travel and Family Stress." *Profile Magazine*, Brussels, 17(1978):12-13.

Johnson, Roger. *Congregations As Nurturing Communities: A Study of Nine Congregations of The Lutheran Church of America.* Division of Parish Services, Lutheran Church of America, 1979.

Kandel, Denise B., and Gerald S. Lesser. *Youth in Two Worlds: United States and Denmark.* Washington, DC: Jossey-Bass, Inc., 1972.

Karssen, Gien. *Her Name Is Woman.* Colorado Springs: NavPress, 1975.

Keen, Sam. *To a Dancing God.* New York: Harper & Row, 1970.

Kohls, L. Robert. *Survival Kit for Overseas Living.* Yarmouth, ME: Intercultural Press, 1984.

Lanto, Sandra. *The Life Planning Workbook for Geographically Mobile Women.* Paris: Women's Institute for Continuing Education at the American College, 1979.

Mansell, Maureen. "Transcultural Experience and Expressive Response." *Communication Education* 30 (April 1981).

Meyer, F.B. *Great Men of the Bible.* Vol. 2. Grand Rapids, MI: Zondervan, 1982.

Miller, Dr. Eric J. "Some Reflections on the Role of the Diplomatic Wife." Privately published for the Werkgroep Vrouwen Buitenlandse Dienst, The Hague, n.d.

Mott, Gordon. "Following a Wife's Move." *New York Times Magazine*, 15 April 1985.

Nash, N. Richard. "The Rainmaker." In *Twelve American Plays 1920-1960*, edited by Richard Corbin and Miriam Balf. New York: Charles Scribner's Sons, 1969.

144

Ogilvie, Lloyd. *A Life Full of Surprises.* Nashville: Abingdon Press, 1969.

Oldenberg, Don. "U.S. Businessmen Abroad Finally Decide the Price of Culture Shock Is Too High." *International Herald Tribune,* 15 August 1984.

"Position Papers Concerning Interests of Foreign Service Employees." Sophie Klubben, The Hague. Manuscript.

Raines, Robert. *To Kiss the Joy.* Waco, TX: Word Books, 1973.

Ramirez, Anthony. "Family on the Move." *Wall Street Journal* 18 February 1979.

Report on the Concerns of Foreign Service Spouses and Families. Forum of the Association of American Foreign Service Women, Washington, DC, March 1977.

Rosellini, Lynn. "The Plight of the Embassy Wife." *New York Times,* 30 April 1981.

Seidenberg, Robert. *Corporate Wives–Corporate Casualties.* New York: American Management Association, 1973.

Statistical Abstract of the U.S., 1988, 108th ed. Washington, DC: U.S. Department of Commerce, Bureau of the Census, 1988.

Sugarman, Dan. *Priceless Gifts: How to Give the Best to Those You Love.* New York: Macmillan Publishing Co., 1978.

Tiger, Lionel. "Is This Trip Necessary? The Heavy Human Costs of Moving Executives Around." *Fortune Magazine* (September 1974): 139.

Turner, Kathy. "Americans Abroad." *Network,* Brussels, 2, no. 2 (1974).

"U.S. Provides Psychiatry for Its Diplomats Abroad." *International Herald Tribune (Paris),* September 1978.

Vandervelde, Maryanne. *The Changing Life of the Corporate Wife.* New York: Mecox Publishing Co., 1979.

Welles, Paddy. *Trials and Tribulations of Transplantation.* Manuscript.

Werkman, Sidney. *Bringing Up Children Overseas.* New York: Basic Books, Inc., 1977.

"When in Rome, It's Sometimes Best to Do As the Romans Do." Provo, UT: Brigham Young University Language and International Research Center, n.d.

Wiesel, Eli. *The Gates of the Forest.* New York: Avon, 1966.

Williams, Margery. *The Velveteen Rabbit.* New York: Avon, 1975.

Wilson, Joan. "Problems of Expatriates." Washington, DC: U.S. Foreign Service Institute, 19 March 1977.

Wink, Walter. *Transforming Bible Study.* Nashville: Abingdon Press, 1980.